The Curious and Amazing Adventures of Maria ter Meetelen

The Slave Market – print, 1684

# The Curious and Amazing Adventures of Maria ter Meetelen

TWELVE YEARS A SLAVE (1731- 43)

*Introduction by Caroline Stone, translated with Karen Johnson*

Hardinge Simpole

Hardinge Simpole Publishing,
The Roan,
Kilkerran,
KA19 8LS,
Scotland,
U.K.

For a complete list of titles, visit
http://www.hardingesimpole.co.uk

e-mail: admin@hardingesimpole.co.uk

Copyright © Caroline E. M. Stone 2010
Translated from the Dutch *Wonderbaarlyke en Merkwaardinge gevallen ven een twaalfjarige slaverny* by Caroline Stone and Karen Johnson
First Published 1748

This edition first published 2010, Copyright © Hardinge Simpole 2010
Introduction © Caroline E. M. Stone 2010
Text copyright © Caroline Stone and Karen Johnson 2010
Cover photograph:
Fez belt mid-19th century © Alexander Stone Lunde 2010.

Every effort has been made to trace possible copyright holders and to obtain their permission for the use of any copyright material. The publishers will gladly receive information enabling them to rectify any error or omission for subsequent editions.

ISBN-13  978 1 84382 217 2 Paperback

All rights reserved. No part of this publication may be reproduced, stored in a retrieval system, or transmitted in any form or by any means, electronic, mechanical, photocopying, recording or otherwise, without the prior permission of the publishers.

# Acknowledgements

I should like to thank the Golden Web Foundation for its financial support during the preparation of this volume, undertaken as part of the Civilizations in Contact Project, Cambridge.

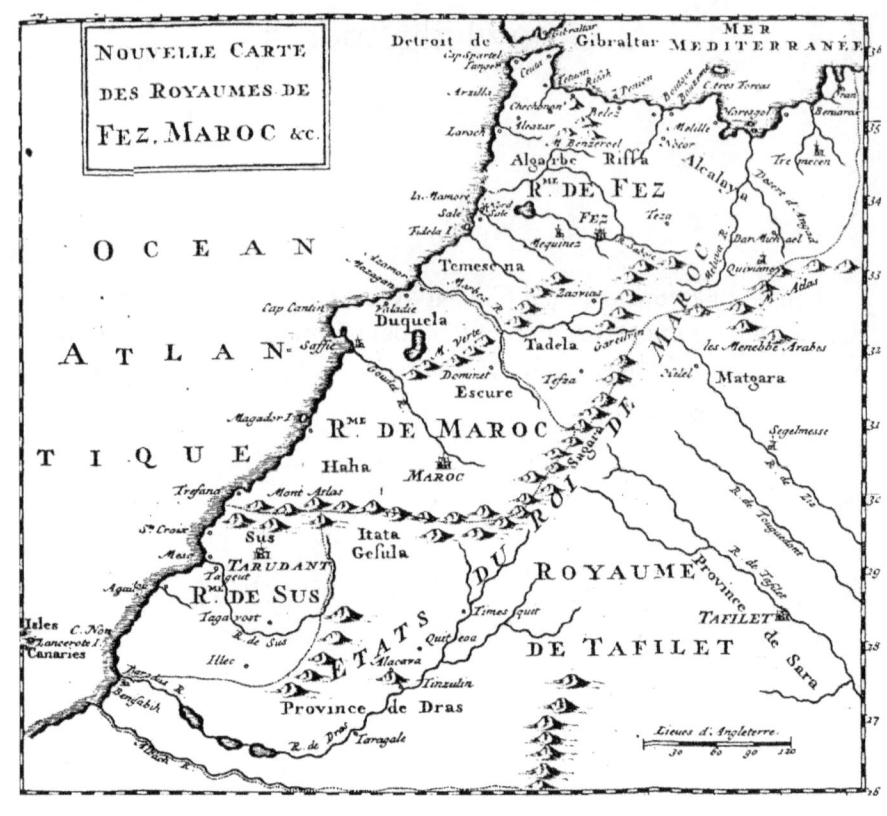

*Map of Morocco, from the French edition of John Braithwaite, The History of the Revolution...in the Empire of Morocco, Amsterdam, 1731. Mequenez (Meknes) is to the west of Fez.*

# Contents

| | |
|---|---|
| Acknowledgements | v |
| **Introduction** | **1** |
| Slaves in North Africa | 1 |
| Slaving | 1 |
| After Capture | 3 |
| The Lives of the Slaves | 5 |
| Redemptions | 10 |
| Renegados | 12 |
| The Abolitionist Movement | 15 |
| Attitudes to White Slavery | 17 |
| The Political Situation in Morocco | 21 |
| The 'Alawi Dynasty | 22 |
| The 'Abīd – the Blacks | 23 |
| Meknès | 25 |
| The Franciscans at Meknès | 26 |
| The Jewish Community at Meknès | 31 |
| Gibraltar | 34 |
| Spain and Holland, Catholic and Protestant | 35 |
| Maria ter Meetelen | 36 |
| Minor Characters | 38 |
| The Mother of Moulay Abdallah - Sayyida Khanāta | 40 |
| The European Slaves of North Africa in Art and Literature | 41 |
| Sources | 41 |
| **Maria ter Meetelen** | **49** |
| The Wanderings of a Transvestite | 49 |
| Corsairs | 51 |
| The Crew Flees | 52 |
| The Corsairs Attack | 52 |
| The Ship is Looted | 54 |
| Arrival at Meknès | 56 |
| Brought Before the King – Moulay Abdallah | 58 |
| The Death of Maria's Husband | 59 |

| | |
|---|---:|
| Choosing a New Husband | 60 |
| Audience with the King | 62 |
| The King's Women Try to Force Maria to Convert | 64 |
| Remarriage | 68 |
| Trouble Makers | 69 |
| Keeping a Tavern | 70 |
| Some Help from the Queen | 71 |
| A Change of Masters | 73 |
| Maria ter Meetelen Protests | 73 |
| Jealousy | 76 |
| Another Christian Woman Makes Trouble | 77 |
| The End of the First Reign of Moulay Abdallah (1731-34) | |
|     The Reign of Moulay Ali al Aredj (1735-6) | 79 |
| Insults and Worse | 80 |
| Summoned by the King | 81 |
| Jean Pusole | 82 |
| Ransoming Slaves – Diplomatic Difficulties | 83 |
| Portuguese Fathers and their Gifts | 85 |
| Maria's Husband Blamed | 86 |
| The Country in Revolt | 87 |
| The second reign of Moulay Abdallah (1736) | |
|     Moulay Muhammad (1736-8) | 88 |
| Four Kings in a Day | 88 |
| Another Tavern | 89 |
| Moulay Muhammad II ben Arbia (1736-38) | 90 |
| Famine and More Slaves Ransomed | 90 |
| Hard Labour | 91 |
| Maria ter Meetelen is in Favour with the King | 92 |
| The King's Violence against his Women | 94 |
| A Wild Boar Fight | 94 |
| Famine, Cannibalism and the Fate of the *Mellah* | 95 |
| Brigands and Other Dangers | 97 |
| Maria ter Meetelen defends her Mistress | 98 |
| Lectures on Astrology and Whales | 99 |
| The Queen Restored to Favour | 99 |
| A Strange Theft Angers the Christian Community | 100 |
| One of the Thieves Converts | 101 |
| The Christians Plot against Maria ter Meetelen | 102 |
| Debate on Astrology | 103 |

| | |
|---|---|
| The Dutch Ambassador | 104 |
| The King Deposed | 105 |
| Accusations Against Maria ter Meetelen | 106 |
| The Reign of Moulay al-Mustadi. | 108 |
| Winemaking | 108 |
| The Third Reign of Moulay Abdallah (1740-41) | 111 |
| Moulay al-Mustadi Deposed | 111 |
| Moulay Zayn al-'Abidīn (1741) | 113 |
| Yet Another King – the Christians Forced to Move to Fez | 113 |
| The Fourth Reign of Moulay Abdallah (1741-42) | 113 |
| Moulay al-Mustadi Proclaimed King Again | 115 |
| Plague | 116 |
| Redemption | 118 |
| Farewells | 119 |
| The Terrible Journey to the Coast | 121 |
| Tétuan and the Plague | 123 |
| The Voyage Home | 125 |
| Attacked by the Spaniards | 126 |
| Trouble over a Goblet | 126 |
| Home at Last | 128 |

**Notes**     **131**

**Appendix 1**     **137**
| | |
|---|---|
| Selected Passages from Al-Nāsirī's *Chronicle* | 137 |
| Moulay 'Abd Allāh [Abdallah] | 138 |
| The King's Mother Goes on the *hajj* | 138 |
| Roots of Disaffection – the 'Abīd and the Berbers | 139 |
| Moulay Abū al-Hasan 'Alī al-'Araj | 140 |
| The Mother of Moulay 'Abd Allāh | 140 |
| The Demands of the 'Abīd and their Consequences | 141 |
| Attack on the Stables | 141 |
| Famine and Urban Insecurity | 142 |
| Food Supplies Brought in by the Christians | 143 |
| Raiding the Storehouses to Pay off the 'Abīd | 143 |
| Moulay 'Abd Allāh's Expropriations in Meknès | 144 |
| Moulay 'Abd Allāh Deposed Again | 145 |
| Moulay Zayn al-'Abidīn | 145 |
| The Death of Khanāta | 146 |
| Manuscripts Sent to the Holy Cities | 146 |

**Appendix 2**     **149**
   Letters Exchanged between the English Ambassador,
       Charles Stewart and the Mother of Moulay Abdallah,
       relating to the Redemption of Captives.     149
   Letter to a queen     150

**Appendix 3**     **157**
   A Partial List of the Sons of the Sultan Moulay
       Ismail as-Samin bin Sharif     157

**Appendix 4**     **161**
   Franciscan Accounts of Meknès at the time of
       Maria ter Meetelen     161

Selected Bibliography     165
Glossary to the Text     169
Index to the Text     171

# List of Illustrations

| | |
|---|---|
| The Slave Market – print, 1684 | ii |
| Map of Morocco, from the French edition of John Braithwaite, *The History of the Revolution…in the Empire of Morocco*, Amsterdam, 1731.. | vi |
| Algiers – early 19th century print. | 4 |
| Negotiating a Redemption - Frontispiece to Pierre Dan, *Historie de Barbarie et ses Corsaires*, 2nd edition, Paris, 1646. | 9 |
| The Harem – watercolour by Aloysius Preziosi, 1851. Reproduced courtesy of the Victoria and Albert Museum, London (SD.832). | 19 |
| The Emperor of Morocco on the Steps of his Palace at Tangiers Surrounded by his Black Guard – anonymous drawing. Reproduced courtesy of the Victoria and Albert Museum, London (SD.1336). | 24 |
| Aerial view of Moulay Ismail's Palace at Meknès – photograph c.1920. | 27 |
| Bab Mellah – entrance to the Jewish Quarter - postcard c.1900. | 33 |
| Mercedarians at Algiers Bargain with the Pasha to redeem Christian Slaves – 1662. | 42 |
| Taking Rais Corsair's Galley – anonymous print, Italy, early 17th century. | 50 |
| Bab Mansour– postcard c.1910. | 57 |
| Ruins of the Dar al-Makhzen – photograph: R. Gréberl, c.1900. | 65 |
| The Grain Market at Meknès – postcard c.1910 | 75 |
| The Armourers Soukh in Meknès – postcard c.1920. | 84 |
| Man and Woman from North Africa – anonymous print, late 16th century. | 93 |
| Bab Berdame – postcard c.1920. | 110 |
| Bab Dar al-Makhzen – postcard c.1910. | 117 |
| Tangiers – anonymous print c.1860 | 120 |
| The Great Mosque at Meknès – postcard c.1900. | 136 |
| The Road to Meknès – anonymous, from John Windus, *A Journey to Meknès*, London: 1725. | 148 |
| Portrait of Moulay Ismail – anonymous, from the German edition of John Windus, *Reise nach Mequinetz*, Hannover : 1726 | 156 |
| Beato Marco d'Aviano, Preaching and Redeeming Captives anonymous print c.1700. | 160 |

# Introduction

In 1731, a young Dutch woman, who had been wandering Europe dressed as a man, had served in a Frisian Dragoon Regiment, and got married in Spain, was captured on her way back to Holland by Barbary pirates. For the next twelve years, she and her husband remained as slaves at Meknès and she wrote an account of her experiences. The following notes are intended to provide a context to the many unfamiliar aspects of the world that she describes.

## Slaves in North Africa

### Slaving

The slave trade in North Africa was big business. It was the maritime equivalent, although on a much smaller scale, of the huge raids, official and unofficial, against Eastern Europe and Russia to supply labour for the Ottoman Empire. Evliya Chelebi, writing in about 1660 leaves no doubt as to the scale:

> "Two hundred and fifty castles and villages were pillaged and nine thousand prisoners taken...The booty was so rich that a slave was sold for ten piastres, an ox for half a piaster, and a sheep for five aspres.."

Or again, among several other descriptions:

> "The castles being situated on high mountains, and in woody tracts, were passed by indulgently, but the villages situated in the plain were all ravaged....Six districts more, the names of which I am ignorant of, shared the common fate of havock...the Ottoman victors were now so loaded with spoils and booty, that it became impossible to carry it all away."[1]

Konstantin Mihailovic[2], captured as a boy, about 1455, and forced to join the Turkish army gives this eye-witness account from his own experience:

> "The Turkish raiders are voluntary - of their own will they ride on expeditions for their livelihood.... They live by means of livestock and raise horses.... If any of them does not want to go on a foray himself, he will lend his horses to others for half (of the spoils); if they win some booty they accept it as good, but if they bring nothing, then they say 'We have no gain, but we have great works of piety, like those who toil with us and ride against the Christians, because we support one another.' And whatever they seize or capture, whether male or female except for boys, they will sell them all for money. The emperor himself will pay for the boys."[3]

Corsairs, on the other hand, captured ships, partly for their cargoes, but largely for their passengers. They might either be enslaved, thus providing the workforce for mining and building projects, and other forms of hard labour, as well as skills, such as gunsmithing and ship-building, that North Africa lacked, or they might be sold or held for ransom. Often what was demanded was cash but, particularly in the later centuries, relatively important captives could be used to extort commercial or diplomatic concessions from the European powers.

Attacks all along the coasts of Europe from Iceland and Ireland to France, Spain and Italy meant that populations had to move inland and away from vulnerable river ports, or go to all kinds of lengths in an effort to protect themselves[4]. The effects of this drain on both the population and the economy – loss of boats and cargoes, ransoms paid, and trade and fishing inhibited – had a serious impact. Cumulatively, the number of people lost was considerable, particularly in view of the population of Western Europe at the time. Figures of well over a million for the period 1500-1800 have been plausibly suggested, for example in Davis, *Christian Slaves, Muslim Masters*, where much useful statistical information is given[5], although many more than this were captured in land raids on Eastern Europe.

The slaving was primarily economic rather than motivated by *jihad*, although the consciousness that there were religious as well financial advantages certainly added to the enthusiasm of many of the slavers, as Mihailovic points out. Slaving, perceived certainly as a right if not a duty, made it particularly difficult for the European powers trying to negotiate, since Muslims frequently claimed that they were not bound to honour agreements made with non-Muslims. In this, they were backed by a number of legal decisions, or *fatwas*, for example that of Abu Sa'id the Grand Mufti of Istanbul, who declared in a mid-17th century response to such a query:

> "God knows everything best. Peace with the infidels is but legal if advantageous to the Muslims, but if it is not, it is not legal at all. As soon as it is useful, it is also allowed to break the peace, be it concluded for a fixed time, or for ever. This is justified by the example of the Prophet...."[6]

This mind-set caused both the Redemptionist Orders and the foreign Consuls endless problems and made setting up functioning international agreements almost impossible. Each mission had to be treated individually and the bargaining depended heavily on the economic and political situation of the hour.

## After Capture

Miss Tully, the sister of the British consul at Tripoli describes the procedure at Algiers in 1784:

> "On their return, this officer [the Dey's inspector] reports to the Dey the conduct of the captain of the cruiser and his crew, and the captain must deliver immediately an account of his success to the government, which claims an eighth part of the prizes, slaves or merchandise, he has taken. The Christian prisoners are brought to the Dey's palace, where the European consuls repair, in order to examine whether any of them belong to their respective nations: if they do, and are only passengers, they can reclaim them; but if it is proved they have served for pay any nation which is at war with Algiers, they cannot be released without paying such ransom as the government may set on them. The Dey has his choice of every eighth, and generally prefers those who are good mechanics to others. The rest, who are left to the owners and captors, are led directly to the besistan, or slave market, where they are appraised and a price is fixed upon each person, from whence they brought

*Algiers – early 19th century print.*

back to the court before the Dey's palace, where they are sold at auction, and whatever is bid above the price set upon them belongs to the government. On the spot where they are sold, these unhappy people have an iron ring fastened on their ankle, with a long or short chain, according as they are supposed to be more or less inclined to escape. Instances do happen of their voluntarily after a time becoming renegados. If any of them can procure money, they are allowed to trade, by paying a high tribute to the Dey, and some in this way subsist and thus remain in slavery. Those who cannot do this and know no trade, are used with great severity: they fare ill and work hard all day, and at night are locked up in public prisons without roofs, where they sleep on the bare ground exposed to the inclemency of the weather, and they are sometimes almost stifled in mud and water. All slaves must go to the public bagnio at night, unless permitted by the favour of the Dey to do otherwise. In town the slaves are seen at the lowest and hardest kind of work, while in the country they are sometimes obliged to draw the plough instead of horses and are in all other respects treated with such inhumanity as would, even there, be severely punished if exercised on brutes."[7]

## The Lives of the Slaves

The lives of slaves in North Africa varied considerably. As Maria ter Meetelen's account shows, the complete uncertainty as to what to expect was one of the things that made their condition so unsettling and distressing. Those for whom handsome ransoms might be paid, or who came at a time when certain political favours were wanted, were apt to be reasonably treated: it was in everyone's interest to keep them alive. The description cited above from Miss Tully gives a much more common pattern.

As a general rule the slaves would be offered to the ruler to take his pick and anyone with useful skills – gunsmith, shipwright, doctor, interpreter and so on – was unlikely ever to be a candidate for ransom. The same was true of attractive women and boys. Surprisingly, in both the case of Maria ter Meetelen and the remarkable Elizabeth Marsh[8], their marriage claims were taken seriously, even though Maria ter Meetelen had been widowed and remarried within a few days, precisely in order to avoid being forced into the harem and Elizabeth Marsh was not married at all. After their liberation, she did in fact marry the man whose wife she had pretended to be.

The greatest immediate danger for the captive was being sold on to the East, where there was an almost insatiable appetite for slaves, especially at Istanbul. Once there, or transferred to the Ottoman provinces, ransom became increasingly unlikely, as numerous writers, including Cervantes, make very clear. Some slaves of course were sold locally and their fate would depend on the nature of their owner.

William Oakley, taken prisoner in June 1639 and a slave for five years before he succeeded in escaping, endured a long period of very harsh treatment before he was finally given to an old gentleman to square a bad debt. Of his last master, he says, honourably:

> "…and if I should be silent here, I should be the most ungrateful wretch living: I found not only pity and compassion, but love and friendship from my new patron, had I been his son, I could not have met with more respect, nor been treated with more tenderness: I could not wish a friend a better condition than I was in – except my bonds."

He argues with himself about the morality of escaping from one who so clearly loved him, but concludes:

> "…fetters of gold do not lose their nature, they are fetters still: had Bajazet's [Bayezid] cage been of gold, as it was of iron, yet it was still a cage; and that was provocation enough to a haughty spirit to beat out his own brains against its bars."[9]

Oakley is also interesting on the psychology of the slave, physically brutalized, constantly frightened – in part by the insecurity of his situation, in part by the tortures inflicted on the disobedient - and generally disorientated, adding:

> "..the truth is, in time we were so habituated to bondage that we almost forgot liberty, and grew stupid and senseless of our slavery, like Issachar "we couched down between our burdens, we bowed our shoulders to bear, and became servants to tribute (Gen. xlix 14, 15)." [10]

He was also aware that sympathy for returning slaves was decidedly limited. Slaving was not perceived as wrong and the centuries from 1600-

1800 marked the height of the European trade in slaves. Those who had been captured tended to be considered, especially in Protestant Europe, as unlucky or imprudent, people who had contrived to cause trouble, and their experiences would be read for entertainment rather than as shedding light on a serious problem or abuse. Oakley foresaw something of this cavalier attitude when he pointed out:

> "However, the reader may afford to run over his eye in an hour that which I ran through in five years; and supposing himself safe upon the amphitheatre, may behold poor slaves combating with beasts below."[11]

This indifference appears, for example, in Samuel Pepys, who casually mentions in his diary on February 8th, 1661, a meeting with two Englishmen who had been slaves at Algiers in a London tavern:

> "….I went to the Fleece Tavern to drink and there we spent till 4 a-clock telling stories of Algier and the manner of the life of Slaves there; and truly, Captn Mootham and Mr Dawes (who have been both slaves there) did make me full acquainted with their condition there. As, how they eat nothing but bread and water. At their redemption they pay so much for the water they drink at the public fountaynes, during their being slaves. How they are beat upon the soles of the feet and bellies at the Liberty of their Padron. How they are all night called into their master's Bagnard, and there they lie. How the poorest men do use their slaves best. How some rogues do live well, if they do invent to bring their masters in so much a week by their industry or theft; and then they are put to no other work at all. And theft there is counted no great crime at all."[12]

But he has almost nothing to say on the subject of slaves or their redemption in his official correspondence from Tangiers.[13]

Nicholas Harding makes the point more forcibly, pointing out that: "Although British emissaries were never encouraged to ransom hostages, it was almost always necessary in order to obtain their release." He remarks how very rarely the English would agree to ransom other nationals, making the occasion described by Maria de Meetelen in August 1734 a particularly unusual one, and he goes on to add:

"British consuls were repeatedly exhorted to minimize the cost of ransoms in general, and their expenses were subject to scrutiny in both Gibraltar and Whitehall. The Government even replaced William Latton in 1750, in part because he had consented to a ransom they had considered exorbitant."[14]

Those who were not important enough to be certain of ransom and were not sold on to private owners or exported, were kept in the notorious slave-barracks or *bagnios*. The term is said to have derived from the slave-quarters in Istanbul located near a major *hammam* or public bath - *bagno* in Italian - the word did not come to mean brothel until slightly later in the century. In theory only single males were kept in the *bagnios*, where conditions varied depending on time and place, but were generally appalling. In the case of families awaiting ransom, efforts were sometimes made to find a more appropriate arrangement, in line with the Islamic view on the protection of women, usually by attaching them to a household, or to the royal palace, as was the case with Maria ter Meetelen.

The unransomed slaves in the *bagnios* were used for hard labour, as Maria ter Meetelen describes, and the death rate was extremely high. The luckier ones, or those who somehow managed to gain access to a little capital, might set up in business, usually by keeping a tavern. Making and selling alcohol and, of course, drinking it was forbidden to Muslims, but non-Muslims were usually given a certain license, especially since the North African states needed and wanted to keep their free European *renegados*, whose drinking generally continued unchecked after conversion. It should be added that non-Muslims were not the only clients of the taverns, as numerous accounts besides the present one indicate.[15]

No fate was seen as worse than being captured by slavers. In a folk song from the early 16th century, found in a manuscript bought by Ogier de Busbecq in Constantinople, a young Greek girl curses the man whom she fears may betray her with the most powerful oath she can conceive:

"If you dare to leave me, if you dare to forget,
May you groan long years in chains among the Turks,
May you find yourself among the Turkish swords and in the hands of the Catalans.[16]
May your flesh be hacked with the double bladed sword
May the Arabs take you, may the Moors capture you,
And may a band of roving Saracens knife you three times…"[17]

A Paris
Chez Pierre Rocolet, Imprimeur & Libraire Ordinaire du ROI.
Au Palais, aux armes de la Ville.
Deuxième édition 1646.
*Avec Privilège du Roi, & Approbation des Docteurs.*

*Negotiating a Redemption – Frontispiece to Pierre Dan, Historie de Barbarie et ses Corsaires, 2nd edition, Paris, 1646.*

## Redemptions

The first problem, of course, was to find where the captive had been taken. This could be time consuming and difficult, but the longer the delay the greater the likelihood of the person, especially if young, vanishing altogether, into a harem, or to the slave markets to the east. For the wealthy, there were a number of options, including the employment of what were essentially trackers; there was then the question of negotiating the release.[18]

Different countries worked out different techniques for redeeming slaves. In Spain, which was one of the countries most severely and systematically affected for geographical reasons, redemption was mainly in the hands of the religious Orders, especially the Mercedarians (Morocco) and the Trinitarians (Tunis and Algiers). They also negotiated for other Catholic captives, particularly from France, since the latter was in origin a French Order, They would collect money from the faithful, who were strongly urged to perform this particular act of charity and bequests often came from ransomed ex-slaves. However, funds were never sufficient and the Fathers did not go on a mission every year. Inevitably, because of this, it was never possible to ransom all the captives. Choices had to be made – the young and vulnerable, those who had no other resources and those most liable to convert typically taking precedence. The terrible strain caused by the knowledge of this choice goes some way to explain the lack of solidarity among the slaves, repeatedly commented on.

Funding aside, organizing a redemption was extremely complicated and might involve diplomats, merchants and professional brokers, often from the Jewish community – anyone, in fact, who had a network of contacts and knew where a bribe or a little discrete pressure would achieve the desired result. Even so, the Orders often found themselves outmanoeuvred and even cheated. On other occasions, particularly in the 13th-15th centuries a direct appeal was sometimes made from one ruler to another, which might or might not prove successful.

The North African rulers frequently demanded Muslim captives in exchange for Christian slaves and while there were occasions on which prisoners of war were available, Muslim slaves were comparatively rare in Europe and, where they did exist, were often compulsorily purchased from their owners in order to be used by the government to procure the release of Christians. Indeed, the gift of a Muslim slave, where one was available, was often the surest way of ensuring the return of a family member, especially in the period before 1700. Nevertheless, as late as 1704, Moulay Ismail was demanding three Muslims for one Frenchman, as a condition of freeing 200 French slaves. The problem was that there were not 600 Muslims captives to be found in France, even taking into account the galleys.[19] This had the unintentional effect of encouraging Christian corsairs to try and seize Muslims, not for use as slaves, but to exchange for Christians.[20]

The economics of the redemptions are very interesting. Buying back a slave was extremely expensive and families were often reduced to beggary in their efforts to ransom their kin. One solution was a loan from merchants or professional go-betweens, which could then be repaid – eventually – through a begging license, which the local authorities, church or secular, normally granted. According to Rodriguez's calculations, it would have taken an unskilled workman twenty five years to beg his ransom, while a sea captain could have managed it from his earnings in a year or less.[21]

The best hope then lay with the Orders. They generally demanded in exchange for ransom some six months of the redeemed captive's time, in which he would help them raise funds for a new redemption by describing his plight and taking part in processions and other rituals.[22] The Catholic Church evolved a whole ceremonial for reintegrating returning ex-slaves into the community, as well as into the faith. It was largely accepted that they if at some point they had converted[23], it was against their will. The public ceremonies and processions also served to show those who had contributed money for the redemption what their generosity had achieved.[24] Processions were also the norm in the Protestant world. John Windus mentions how the British captives ransomed in 1712 "went in Procession to St Paul's to return Thanks to Almighty God for their Happy Deliverance." Altogether, this was a very small price to pay, compared to all the other options available to the poor. It also gave the ex-slave an opportunity to re-enter the community less brutally than by returning to his village in poor health and a beggar, only to find his wife married to someone else, or all his family gone and no one left who even recognized him.

The ransom of slaves from Protestant countries was not as systematic and was more often negotiated by merchants or resident consuls, naval officers sent for the purpose, or diplomatic missions, frequently with the intervention of the local Jewish merchants. Maria ter Meetelen's account mentions all these elements. Ransoming their own captives was always a very high priority for the Jewish community and money was usually collected for this purpose by the synagogues[25]. In some, there was even a special "overseer of the captives", originally in Spain and Portugal also concerned with negotiating for those seized by the Inquisition, and known as the *Parnas dos Cautivos*. It would be extremely interesting to know what arrangements were made for the vast numbers of slaves from the Orthodox world to the East. The few instances that I have come across, other than repurchase by the Russian government, have relied on personal intervention, often by an Armenian merchant, as in the case related by Miss Tully.[26]

## *Renegados*

The Catholic Redemptionist Orders put much stress on the dangers of conversion, especially if slaves were to feel themselves abandoned and without hope of ransom, and for that reason those felt to be in danger of apostatizing were given precedence in the redemptions. It should be remembered that the issue was not simply slavery: apostasy implied spiritual loss and no hope of eternal Redemption.

The Protestants were also concerned, but for somewhat different reasons. John Braithwaite, writing in 1728-9, after a mission to redeem British captives at Meknès, leaves sentiment and salvation firmly aside:

> "And here it may not be improper to observe, of what advantage it is to our Trade in general, to redeem Captives; and tho it puts the Government to some Expence, yet it answers in the End. The People generally taken into this Country are Sea-men, among which Number are Carpenters, Caulkers, Sail-makers &c. if these men were once made desperate, by knowing they were to dwell in Captivity for Life, it would be a great temptation to them to turn Moors; and they have sometimes had between 3 and 400 of our Sailors in Captivity, so that in time they might be able in a great measure to cruise upon us with our own People; however, they might be so assisted in the fitting, building, repairing, and navigating their Ships, that they might be made much more troublesome to us than they are."[27]

In some cases conversion was forced. This varied very much, depending on time and place. On the one hand, the Muslim view was that conversion was by definition good and trying to compel it a religious duty; on the other, there were often mixed feelings about the reliability of *renegados*, to say nothing of the economic loss of labour or potential ransom when a slave decided to convert and had, at least theoretically, to be freed. This was a vexed question and the maintaining of blacks, who were generally Muslim, in a state of slavery was deeply disapproved of by such men as the chronicler al-Nāsirī (see Appendix 1), not on racial or humanitarian grounds, but as a point of Islamic law.

Individuals also had very different reactions to the experience of apostasy, ranging from compliance to deep guilt to indifference. Johann Schiltberger captured, aged 14. at the disastrous battle of Nicopolis in 1396 was spared death because of his youth, but enslaved and forced to convert – he describes the process. He was subsequently slave to three of the great figures of the age: the Ottoman Sultan Bayazid, Timur and Timur's son Shah Rukh. Nevertheless, when he finally succeeded in escaping thirty years later, he instantly returned to his faith of origin, went home and sat down to dictate his memoirs.[28]

Slaves, then, were often forced, or at least heavily pressured to convert, as Maria ter Meetelen describes, while others did so in order to survive. Children, of course, had no choice, as in the scene in Miguel de Cervantes *Trato de Argel*[29], no doubt drawn from his own experiences during his five years captivity in Algiers[30]. In the play, realization gradually dawns on the little boys that they will be parted from their parents and forcibly converted to Islam. The parents know that their children will probably be offered for sale in Istanbul and so lost for ever. The best they could hope would be that the boys would escape castration, since they were the right age for the operation and eunuchs, especially white eunuchs, fetched a much higher price.

A certain proportion of the Europeans encountered were *renegados* by choice, men who had left their countries because they were in trouble with the law, or in order to better their condition in North Africa, which was a land of opportunity for a mercenary or anyone with skills. It was also a haven for all the corsairs, who had profited from the long-running hostilities among England, the Netherlands and Spain, and who suddenly found themselves not only unemployed, but also on the wrong side of the law, when peace was negotiated in the first years of the 17$^{th}$ century. Resentment against the society of their birth, the need to prove their loyalty to the society they had joined, and doubtless in some cases the notorious fanaticism of the convert, meant that *renegados* were often crueller and more feared than those born Muslim.

This served to sharpen the terror of conversion expressed by Maria ter Meetelen and her fellow slaves. The temptation was clearly great. As

Miss Tully remarks, writing at the end of the 18th century: "I have before observed to you, that when Christian slaves become *renegados*, they often hold the highest offices in Turkey and Barbary."[31]

It was not simply the total rejection that conversion implied of country, family, culture and faith, that horrified the Christian community, but also the fact that these men brought their technical skills and local knowledge to the enemy, as Braithwaite pointed out. In the early 16th century, for example, John Ward of Favisham and a Dutchman, Simon Danser of Dordrecht, taught the Barbary pirates how to build square-rigged European-type ships, faster, more stable and with a greater range than the local lateen-rigged vessels, thus greatly increasing the scope of their attacks.[32]

A number of the most famous slave raids were carried out by *renegados*. Jan Jansen was a prime example. Originally from Haarlem in the Netherlands, he began his career as a Dutch privateer harassing Spanish shipping, but after the peace found there was not enough money in it and by a long and complicated route moved his centre of operations to Algiers. There he married and converted to Islam – he already had a wife and children in Holland – taking the name of Murat Rais. Soon after, he moved to Salé, on the Atlantic coast of Morocco, a city that lived from piracy, and by his good advice made it so wealthy that when it declared itself an independent republic, he was elected first admiral or *ra'is* - leader.

In 1622, he took an expedition up the English Channel and in 1627, he bought a Danish slave to serve as pilot and headed for Iceland where he and his men raided Reykjavik, killing 36 and carrying off between two and three hundred people, a high percentage of its population at the time, to be sold as slaves at Salé. One of them not only survived but apparently wrote an account of his experiences.[33] The sack of Baltimore in Ireland, on the 20th of June, 1631, well-known from the famous ballad, was probably also led by Jan Jansen. Contemporary accounts survive, as well as a list of the people carried off with their ages and occupations, which could serve for almost any coastal town in Europe that had suffered a slave raid.[34]

Other conversions were matters of expediency. John Braithwaite gives a couple of examples, which must have been very typical:

"Before we left this town, a Spaniard turned Moor, and was clothed by the Saint A la Moresco[35]: I spoke to this Fellow, and ask'd him the Reason of it; he told me that he had been a Soldier of the

Garrison at Ceuta, but being tired of that Life had deserted to the Moors, in hopes to be free and return to Europe, but finding his Mistake, and that he was to be a Slave to the Moors, he had deserted from them, and was travelling toward Tangier, in hopes to have concealed himself and swam off, on board some French or English Vessel, of which there is generally one in the Road; but being pursued, he was taken, and for fear of being put to Death he turned Moor, and was to march with us to Mequenez [Meknès] to be put among the rest of the Renegadoes."[36]

And again:

"This Day an Englishman, his name Daws, a Norfolk man, made himself acquainted with the Servants: he turned Renegado about 46 years ago, and is about 60 Years of Age; and has had two Wives in this Country. We sent for him, and found him a very sensible Man, and by having lived so long in the Country, was capable of giving very good Account of things: He told us the Reason of his turning Moor, was the late King's threatning to kill him, but after a better Acquaintance, he owned it was the Temptation of living an easy Life and being his own Master; for he said in those Days there were no Hopes of being redeemed, as has been practised since."[37]

## The Abolitionist Movement

Although the moral implications of the institution of slavery had been much discussed down the centuries and Charles V of Spain, in the *Leyes de Indias* of 1542, had declared all native inhabitants of his New World empire free[38] – although not free from punitive exactions of labour - at the period of Maria ter Meetelen's captivity the anti-slavery movement was still in the future.

In fact, it is interesting to note the change of attitude that was taking place in Europe between the time at which Maria ter Meetelen and Elizabeth Marsh[39] - captured in 1756 and by great good fortune ransomed within a few days - were writing and the period of Miss Tully, whose *Letters from Tripoli* dates from 1783-93. Neither Maria ter Meetelen, who endured many years of slavery, nor Elizabeth Marsh who risked it, express abhorrence of it as an institution. They, obviously, did not want to be enslaved, but they did not see it as something intrinsically evil. By the end of the century, however, Miss Tully, although she herself was never in specific danger, repeatedly expresses her horror at it - an indication of the evolution in public perception wrought by the Abolitionist movement which had been gathering force during the second half of the 18th and into the 19th century.

The situation was somewhat different in southern Europe, where far more people had been affected by slave raids for a much longer period and where loss of a family member or the sight of a returned captive begging to repay his ransom had sensitized the general population to the implications of slavery, at least for themselves - although there was little impetus to abolish it as a general principal, in spite of intermittent exhortations by the Catholic Church.

Abolition was to be violently opposed not only by slave-owners in the Americas, but also across much of the Muslim world.[40] In the mid-19th century, the Ottoman Empire, not loath to join the West in its campaign against slavery for a number of reasons, was immediately denounced by the *sharīfs* of Mecca, who issued a *fatwa* – religious decree – condemning all those who wished to abolish slavery:

> "The Turks have become renegades. It is obligatory to make war against them and against those who follow them. Those who are with us are for heaven and those who are with them are for hell. Their blood is lawful and their goods are licit."[41]

In other words, the Turks could be killed or enslaved with impunity and their possessions impounded because they had considered the possibility of abolishing the institution of slavery, permitted to Muslims according to the *shari'a*.

At about the same date, an Abolitionist delegation to Morocco, where the ruling house claimed *sharīfi* genealogy, did not have any great success. Their speech ended:

> " 'We come not to your Excellency with force of arms — this could not be just; we use only moral persuasion. Our religion disapproves of compulsion in all such affairs. But I can assure your Excellency that the English people will never cease, though all nations be against them, as long as God Almighty holds them up as a people, to endeavour in every possible way, to persuade and convince the world that the traffic in human beings is a great crime.'

The Governor replied in these terms:

> 'Your mission is against our religion, I cannot entertain it or think of it, in any way whatever. If, in other countries, the traffic in slaves is contrary to the religion of those countries, in this it is not; here it is lawful for us to buy and sell slaves. Mahomet, our Prophet, has authorized us to do this.'"[42]

## Attitudes to White Slavery

Attitudes to European enslavement are in some ways surprising. The stance of the Catholic Church has already been discussed. The secular authorities, on the other hand, were uneven in their response and often surprisingly casual, given that the impact on those areas regularly affected by slaving was considerable. Not only did many families, especially in coastal areas, have direct experience of loss, but the economic backlash would have been a constant reminder, as households were made destitute and communities impoverished. Efforts at mutual protection also shaped social organization and, inevitably, long-term attitudes towards the aggressors. Religious wars were perceived as continuing, when the real issues were neither *jihad* nor crusade, but manpower and money. The experience even left traces in the language: the Spanish expression "*Hay moros en la costa!*" – Moors in view! – now used to warn of any imminent danger, once meant exactly what it said.

In Northern Protestant Europe the mindset tended to be different and it is interesting to consider why black slavery was given so much more attention than white. It is partly because, from about 1800, white slavery began to decline, for complex reasons, including the hardening stance of the Western powers towards the slavers. This was largely the result of the Abolitionist movement, which incidentally benefited the Christians, although it was aimed at the African slave trade, the primary raiders and dealers in both cases being Muslim. Colonization, stimulated in part by a desire to end the problem of slave raids, in both North Africa and the eastern edges of the Russian Empire also had its effect. Another important element in the attitude of Northern Europe was that the Europeans enslaved were predominantly southern Catholics and eastern Orthodox Christians, two groups for which Northern Europe had little sympathy.

Another point is worth considering: for southern Europe, slavery was perceived as a misfortune that could happen to anyone and therefore a considerable degree of empathy was normal and expected. For countries like England, on the other hand, rising imperial powers, slavery was not something that should happen to "us" – it was something that happened to "them"[43]. One's co-nationals enslaved were therefore an embarrassment and while some effort might be made to rescue them for practical reasons, or to avoid loss of face, it was felt better that the whole subject should be ignored or forgotten whenever possible. The victim-oriented view of history was not yet dominant: when the French took Algiers from the Ottomans in 1830, the *bagnios* were pulled down in the course of urban redevelopment. The idea of preserving them as a monument to their co-nationals suffering would never have occurred.

The cause of white slavery was also done a great disservice by the *orientaliste* fantasies of the Victorian period.[44] Indeed, the term was to become almost a joke. Westerners were seduced into a romantic view of Muslim slavery by the descriptions of travellers who naturally only saw the most glamorous and attractive sides. This is how the harem of the Shah of Iran appeared to Elizabeth McNeill in the early 19th century:

> "Nothing could exceed the splendour, the magnificence, the dazzling richness and brilliance of the scene. The slave girls were blazing in diamonds and rubies, brocade and spangles. Their dresses, originally of the richest stuffs, were so closely embroidered with pearls and precious stones that little else could be seen. Their hair hung loose and their heads were ornamented in various ways with jewels."[45]

On this basis, it was decided, quite arbitrarily, that slavery in Islam was a pleasant and desirable experience and the reality was masked by thousands of paintings, many of them what today would be called soft porn, celebrating the delights of the slave market and the harem. This titillating view of unlimited sexual opportunity – for men – left out of count the vast majority of slaves who were not harem favourites, but working in menial jobs, in mines and quarries or in the galleys. Women who had experienced slavery at first hand or recorded the experience of those who had, such as Florence Baker[46], Miss Tully or indeed Maria ter Meetelen, were well aware of the human suffering involved, for which pretty clothes would not compensate. However, the myth that women, particularly from Eastern Europe and the Caucasus, eagerly chose slavery fitted well with many of the other prejudices of the age and devalued

*The Harem* – watercolour by Aloysius Preziosi, 1851. Reproduced courtesy of the Victoria and Albert Museum, London (SD.832).

the whole subject of European slavery. No doubt there were girls who preferred life in the harem to the harsh conditions of a mountain village, and parents who of necessity sold their children, but the Italian traveller, Pietro della Valle, who was in Isfahan about 1620 and negotiated with Shah Abbas on behalf of the Christians, shows the phenomenon in a rather different light:

> "Today Persia proper, Kirman or Carmania, Mazan-deran on the Caspian Sea and many other lands of this empire are all full of Georgian and Circassian inhabitants. Most of them remain Christian to this day, but in a very crude manner, since they have neither priest nor minister to tend them. . . .. There is no grandee who does not want all his wives to be Georgian, because it is a very handsome race, and the king himself has his palace full of them. . . . It would be too long to narrate all that has passed in this miserable migration, how many murders, how many deaths caused by privation, how many seductions, rapes and acts of violence, how many children drowned by their own parents or cast into rivers through despair, some snatched by force from their mother's breasts because they seemed too weak to live and thrown down by the wayside and abandoned there to be food for wild beasts or trampled underfoot by the horses and camels of the army, which marched for a whole day on top of dead bodies; how many sons separated from their fathers, wives from their husbands, sisters from their brothers, and carried off to distant countries without hope of ever meeting again. Throughout the camp, men and women were sold on this occasion much cheaper than beasts, because of the great number of them."[47]

There was yet another aspect of the attitude to the two types of slavery, besides the very valid point that European slaves had some hope of ransom – perhaps a one in twenty chance – whereas African slaves had none. The Low Church, which was so prominent in the Abolitionist movement, was very concerned with the wickedness of slave trading and slave owning, as well as the misery of the slaves. In the case of white slaves, the traders and owners were Muslim and so one half of the impetus to outrage was lost. In the case of black slaves, the role of the blacks in selling their own prisoners of war and tribal enemies and that of the Muslims as both dealers and large-scale consumers was generally glossed over. It was the actions of the Christians that were perceived as important, because for them slaving was wrong, whereas for the others it was not. This led to a very marked tendency to contrast the evils of American slave owning with the practice believed to be benign in the Muslim world. The view is simplistic. While it is true that because slavery was legal in Islam, a slave theoretically had more rights, enforcing them was not easy and the possibility of wealth and advancement for a few in no way mitigated the trauma of losing family, home, language, culture and faith, as well as liberty, for the great majority. A house slave in either culture might well enjoy a measure of respect, but the experience for a plantation slave or one in the salt mines of Taudenni would have been equally brutal.

## The Political Situation in Morocco

The political situation at the time that Maria ter Meetelen was in Morocco was one of extreme complexity and this is only the barest outline. The death of Moulay Ismail, who had to some extent imposed unity, left the country prey to wars of succession among his many children, as the section on the 'Alawi dynasty and Appendix 3 make clear.

There were, however, added complications. Morocco was in origin a Berber country, which had then experienced successive waves of Arab invaders, and the Berbers in turn were of different tribal confederations, often at war among themselves. Very roughly, the cities tended to be Arab, with a considerable admixture of Jewish residents, while the countryside was largely Berber. This resulted in a situation, not uncommon in Muslim lands and elsewhere, but formalized in Morocco: that the ruler's control did not extend outside the main cities – this was *blad al-makhzen*, government land – while the rest of the country, where tax could not be gathered or law enforced, was *blad al-siba* – land beyond control.[48] This meant that the countryside was in a virtually permanent state of revolt, or low-level civil war, with a very negative impact on trade and general prosperity.

Three further issues complicated the situation and contributed to the ungovernableness of the country. Firstly, the black slave army brought in by Moulay Ismail, which frequently ransacked both towns and countryside and was generally at odds with the Berbers - see the section on the *'Abīd* and the passages from al-Nāsirī's *Chronicle*. Secondly, the foreign enclaves, some of which had been reconquered by Moulay Ismail, such as Larache and Tangiers, but others still survived in the 18th century: Ceuta, Mazagan (El Jedida), Melilla…Thirdly, while Ottoman ambitions to extend their influence west from Algiers never succeeded, their presence on the borders of Morocco added another element to the already unstable political mixture.

## The 'Alawi Dynasty

The 'Alawi *sharīfs* – or descendants of the family of the Prophet Muhammad – became politically important from the early 15th century, for their *jihad* against the Portuguese and their association with the Dala'iyya religious confraternity.[49] In the 1660s, Moulay Rashid managed to assert his ascendancy over the tribes; his descendants still rule Morocco. The religious authority of the 'Alawis was fundamental to their maintaining power. The title Moulay or Mulay, meaning "lord" or "master" is given to all *sharīfs* and was adopted by the 'Alawis as their title, in preference to *malik* – king – or sultan both, strictly speaking, disapproved of in Islam.

Moulay Ismail[50] (1672-1727) was the second ruler of the 'Alawi Dynasty in Morocco. After being defeated on several fronts, notably by the Ottoman Protectorate of Algiers, he decided to form his own personal army of black slaves, the 'Abīd al-Bukhari, which eventually numbered some 150 000 men. This force enabled him to drive the Europeans from several of their coastal strongholds and wage numerous campaigns against the Berber tribes, thus unifying the country. He moved the capital from Fez to Meknès, where he built a magnificent imperial city, partly in conscious rivalry with Louis XIV, with whom he was in diplomatic contact. Notoriously, the workforce constructing the walls was largely composed of Christian slaves; the stone was in part mined from the classical cities of Volubilis and Chellah[51], outside Rabat.

Moulay Ismail had many wives, among them allegedly an Irishwoman[52], and numerous sons, several of whom rebelled, or were believed to be plotting rebellion, against their father. They were executed, using the same pitiless tactics that led to the deaths of some 30 000 disobedient subjects and kept Moulay Ismail in power for 45 years. After Moulay Ismail's death, his surviving sons fought among themselves for decades, giving rise to the extremely confusing situation described by Maria ter Meetelen. Often one son would be ruling in one city, while his half brothers had carved out fiefdoms in other parts of the country, so that in effect there was no universally recognized ruler.

Different sources give different numbers of sons, and names and dates also vary considerably. The speed of regime change, especially during the years that Maria ter Meetelen was in Meknès was dizzying. To give a slight feeling for the political background of the narrative, a partial list of the sons of Moulay Ismail, and the Sultans of Morocco from his death until the departure of Maria ter Meetelen has been added in Appendix 3.

### The 'Abīd – the Blacks[53]

A common pattern in Islamic states was the creation of a slave army to uphold the power of the ruler. Isolated from the population by their state of slavery and hence lack of tribe, family, roots or economic base, and hated by it for their position as military enforcers, tax collectors and also for their ethnic difference (black, Turkic or European renegade), a slave army had little choice but loyalty to the ruler – but not always the ruler who had originally recruited them.

Moulay Ismail (fl.1672-1727), after a number of humiliating defeats by his enemies – unpacified tribes, Ottomans Turks and, along the coast, European interlopers – decided to form his own army of black and *haratīn* slaves, acquiring some 15 000 by compulsory purchase, to which were added women for the slaves to marry and breed replacements. A camp was set up for them at Mashra al-Ramal (mentioned by Maria ter Meetelen as Romel) between Meknès and Salé, and they swore allegiance on the work of the great Muslim traditionist al-Bukhārī, *al-Saḥīḥ*, which, according to al-Nāsirī, became the slave army's battle standard. For this reason, they were known as *'Abīd al-Bukhārī* – or the Blacks of al-Bukhārī, a name which added religious authority to their other powers, this being a very important element in the control strategy of the 'Alawi dynasty.

Unlike many slave armies, those of Moulay Ismail were trained as an occupying as well as fighting force and were established in more than twenty *kasbahs* about the countryside, to intimidate the population and control the routes. The chronicler, al-Nāsirī (see Appendix 1) was unequivocally pro-'Alawi, but he gives numerous examples of the extreme suffering inflicted on the civilian population by the 'Abīd, both under Moulay Ismail, as he became more and more confident of his position and hence indifferent to popular opinion, and his successors.[54]

The 'Abīd were financed by taxes – their wars were normally presented as *jihad* – income from piracy and the redemption of Christian slaves; and permission to loot both cities, and tribal territories. If they were displeased by their treatment, or if sufficient money were not forthcoming, they would depose the ruler and choose an alternative. This was particularly true in the

*The Emperor of Morocco on the Steps of his Palace at Tangiers Surrounded by his Black Guard – anonymous drawing. Reproduced*

chaotic thirty years during which Moulay Ismail's sons battled for power after his death, as both Maria ter Meetelen and al-Nāsirī describe. By this stage, the 'Abīd had ceased to be an effective, if cruel, stabilizing force and had become a liability for their masters and a terror for the citizens.

## Meknès

Meknès[55] stands on the edge of the Middle Atlas in an area of good agricultural land – hence its Arabic name: Miknās al-Zaytūn – Meknès of the Olives. The name Miknās comes from Berber Miknāsa tribe, who settled there in the 10$^{th}$ century during the great migrations of the Zenata Berber confederation. Little is known of its early history, but probably by the 11$^{th}$ century the local *kasbah*, or fortified village, had expanded to form a walled town. Meknès' fortunes varied through the Middle Ages, but it was very important as a religious centre with *zāwiyyas* for many Muslim brotherhoods, especially the Isawiyya. *Zāwiyyas* were establishments for religious retreat and instruction. They were often attached to the tomb of a *marabout* or saint, and were centres of mystic devotion rather than intended to promote orthodox religious education like the *madrasas* in eastern Islam. Meknès also had a considerable Jewish population, greatly increased by Andalusian immigrants from the end of the 14$^{th}$ century.

Moulay Ismail (c.1645-1727), who had been sent to live at Meknès before his accession, transformed the city by choosing it as his capital. Not only did he wish to avoid the entrenched tribal and political affiliations of Fez and Marrakech, but he also wanted a city that he felt to be truly his own and loyal only to him. For fifty years, he engaged in an enormous building project to convert it into a royal city. John Windus, visiting it in 1721 wrote:

> "The Emperor is wonderfully addicted to Building; yet it is more a Question whether he is more addicted to that, or pulling down, for they say if all his Buildings were now standing, by a moderate Computation, they would reach to Fez…"[56]

His palaces, especially the one for his women, the Dar Kbira (Great House), were vast, but rambling, defended by a series of walls and bastions. It may be the place mentioned in Maria ter Meetelen's descriptions. Besides palaces and fortifications, there were, of course, mosques, storehouses, arsenals, vast granaries and stables, as well as markets, *hammams* and all the other structures normally found in an Islamic city of the period.

To the southwest of the city, stood Madinat-al-Riyad, where officials had their palaces and there were also government buildings and inns - primarily for merchants. Moulay Ismail built another palace there, as well as a school and a library. In 1732-3, Moulay Abdallah, one of Moulay Ismail's sons, had Madinat al-Riyad destroyed by Christian slaves, apparently on a whim, leaving only the main gateway, Bab al-Khamis – al-Nāsirī in his *Chronicle* describes the event (see Appendix 1).

The entrances to the palace were, following North African tradition, tortuous, for reasons of security, but also because the building was extended repeatedly in the course of Moulay Ismail's reign with no real master plan. Maria ter Meetelen's confused descriptions of crossing the palace are therefore quite consistent with the architectural reality.

Moulay Ismail took great personal interest in his city, allegedly hoping to rival Louis XIV's creation at Versailles. He imposed forced labour on the tribes, but relied above all on Christian slaves and, to some extent, skilled *renegados* for its construction.

### The Franciscans at Meknès[57]

Unlike many North African ports, including Tangiers, which were Christian from Roman times, and even some inland cities, such as Marrakech, where, after the martyrdom of the first Franciscan preachers in 1220, a church was built and a bishopric established in 1225, Meknès had no Christian past. As pirate strongholds, such as Salé, lost their independence, all the slaves became the property of the ruler and, in about 1673, Moulay Ismail decided to concentrate the Christians at Meknès, where he was building his new capital. He also had the Franciscans move their base there, in order to minister to the slaves and provide medical care.

The slaves were kept in vast humid subterranean chambers near the stables with the sewers running through them. This was the *mazamorra*, the local version of the cone-shaped underground storerooms, *matmura* typical of the Berber areas. *Matmura* - impossible to escape from unless a rope were let down - were used as holding pens for slaves in many parts of North Africa and in the Muslim Kingdom of Granada. Turning down Moulay Ismail's offer of a "solitary and pleasant place", the Franciscans established themselves among the slaves, sharing their lives and caring for them as best they could. It was, according to Koehler, " reminiscent

*Aerial view of Moulay Ismail's Palace at Meknès – photograph c.1920.*

of the catacombs". Judging from the Franciscan accounts, which describe the conditions in some detail, the *mazamorra* was near the present-day Rue Rouamzine.[58]

The *mazamorra* was destroyed when Moulay Ismail wanted to extend his palace and the Franciscans were allowed to rebuild in an area known as Ka'a al-Ward - Quarter of the Roses – between the west wall of the old Dar al-Maghzen and Bab Tizimi. This was the Royal Convent of the Immaculate Conception of Our Lady. The Christian slaves were given permission to build whatever shelters they could and their neighbourhood was divided into Spanish, English, French and Portuguese quarters, reflecting the nations most affected by slave raids from the Barbary Coast. Following normal practice in Muslim cities, each "nation" had a headman, who acted as a liaison with the local officials and was responsible for the behaviour of his co-nationals. In addition, there was one person appointed as head of all the foreign slaves.

The main church, Our Lady of Meknès, with carvings and a fine painting of the Virgin, stood in the Spaniards' quarter, since it had been paid for by them, and it was from there that the processions, which even the Muslim population enjoyed watching, started out. There was also an infirmary that could care for a hundred sick, generously supported by the Spanish and less so by the French, and care was also given to any locals who asked for it. Successive rulers made much use of the Fathers' skills and especially the medicines they prepared in their dispensary.

Details of the Convent have survived: the Fathers had paper and ink in their cells, and sand to serve as blotting paper. On occasion, even chocolate and tobacco were allowed, and they were hospitable to passing foreigners, including Protestants, although John Windus tells us:

> "....we dined with the Prior, who, I believe, did his best, but his Cooks being Spaniards, the Victuals were sadly drest for our taste, and his Wine very bad..."[59]

However, the Convent cat had a little bell sent by a well-wisher from Cadiz.

The Franciscan Archives include volumes recording births, marriages and deaths, as well as numerous reports and letters, which give a fascinating insight into the lives of both Fathers and slaves at Meknès, and also statistical information.[60] Judging by these records, there seem to have been about a thousand European slaves at Meknès in the late 17th-early 18th centuries, except after the fall of the Spanish city of Larache in 1689, when numbers rose to above 3000. This tallies with the numbers given by John Windus for the year 1721:

> "The Ambassador had the good Success to embark 296 English, being what were left alive, (and had not turned Moors) of those who had been taken in about seven Years War. At our coming to Mequinez there were reckoned to be above 1100 Christians, about 300 of which were English, not including 19 who had turned Moors; 400 Spaniards, 155 Portuguese, 152 French, 69 Dutch, 25 Genoese, and three Greeks of the Morea; some of all these different nations had turned Moors, thereby for ever losing hope of Redemption.
> Nor are the Expectations of the rest much better, it being very unlikely there will ever be Peace between the Moors and any of the fore-mentioned Nations; tho' there are now and then Treaties of Redemption for them, the former of which have Consuls in the Chief Ports, notwithstanding the State of War they are in; and the latter very often a couple of Fryars residing in Tetuan, besides those I have mentioned belonging to the Convent at Mequinez."[61]

The secret of the English success on this and other occasions, was that they were supplying the rulers with war materiel: – "…Powder for part of their Ransom being arrived from Gibraltar…" - something forbidden to official Catholic missions.

The number of slaves at Meknès at any one time was relatively modest, compared to Algiers, where there were an estimated 7000 Dutch[62], besides other nationals, in the mid-17th century. The figures, of course, do not reflect the numbers of captives immediately sent on to the major slave-markets, particularly at Istanbul, and who therefore never entered the accounting of the redemptions.

Among other records kept by the Fathers, there is one that lists the small number of *renegados* who, risking death, made a formal but secret retraction of their conversion to Islam. This had to take place before ten Christian witnesses, who were not related to them. One woman, Catalina Dias, has a particularly striking story. Her mother, Maria da Silva, a servant, was travelling with her mistress from Lisbon to the convent that the lady was about to enter as a nun, when they were captured and taken to Meknès. Treated much as Maria ter Meetelen describes, Maria's mistress accepted Islam and entered the harem. Maria da Silva refused so energetically and even resisted being burned on her arms and breasts that she was allowed to go back to the Christian community. There, again like Maria ter Meetelen, the Fathers quickly married her to a co-national, Joseph Dias, captured at Larache. He was valuable for his skills, especially making gunpowder, so that when in 1718 he dared to ask for his freedom, Moulay Ismail, in a rage at the thought of losing him, had his throat cut. The Fathers added, regretfully, that he had had no time to confess and the night before had been playing cards, cheating a little and blaspheming: "May I lose my head if I lie!" Joseph and Maria's daughter Catalina was forcibly converted and taken to the harem. She is one of those who appear in the record of secret Christians after Moulay Ismail's death. Mother and daughter seem to have been freed in one of the Portuguese redemptions – possibly the one mentioned by Maria ter Meetelen.[63]

The Fathers were unable to save Joseph Dias, but they frequently tried to intervene on behalf of Christians caught up in the rages of Meknès' rulers. Their efforts were not always gratefully received and sometimes captives resentful at not obtaining the aid they hoped for informed against them and, often successfully, stirred up trouble with the Moroccan authorities.

It is counter-intuitive how little solidarity there seems to have been among the slaves, even those of the same nationality, as Maria ter Meetelen makes bitterly clear. Other first person accounts, as well as those of the Fathers, remark on the amount of jealousy, backbiting and dangerous trouble-making, even going as far as attempts to sabotage redemptions by those who had not been included. John Windus gives a particularly striking example of this, where the negotiations were only saved by the intervention of Moulay Abdallah's mother (see Appendix 2).

Clearly, the stress of the situation was almost intolerable. Besides being torn from their world, forcibly separated from family and friends, living very often in appalling conditions, with hunger and hard labour, the slaves were in a constant state of fear. This was deliberate on the part of large-scale owners: terrified slaves were docile and it was worth killing one occasionally to ensure the subjection of the rest. Violent deaths were common, whether the ruler on a whim wanted to try out his gun or whether, for some unspecified offence, a slave would literally be thrown to the lions. Then there was always the fear that someone would give way and "turn Turk". This not only weakened and demoralized the community: statistics indicate that every conversion had very serious repercussions on the social fabric of the slaves, but also put an often particularly vindictive and knowledgeable enemy in the opposite camp.[64]

Almost worse than the fear was the hope. The uncertainty surrounding the redemptions – would they come? Would there be money? Would they be chosen? It has been calculated that not more than one in twenty, or in particularly favoured periods one in ten, were in fact rescued. It is hardly surprising that, as one Franciscan points out, the characters of the slaves became "embittered, despairing and envious."[65] It would be extremely interesting to compare what is known of behaviour in the Christian slave communities of North Africa with records of the experiences in the prison camps and gulags of our own time.

Some years after Maria ter Meetelen left, the Fathers ran into trouble from accusations made by the Christians over a redemption and were beaten and imprisoned. Later that year, the Convent, Church, Infirmary and other buildings belonging to the Franciscans were destroyed in the earthquake that levelled Lisbon. The original letters from the Father Guardian have not survived, but in a later compilation a document recorded as dating from November 8th, 1755, describes the total destruction of all their possessions in Meknès, presumably referring to the November 1st Lisbon earthquake, rather than the more local quake of November 18th. [66]

The mission never fully recovered. There was some rebuilding, but the decreasing number of captives – and hence funding - and increasing levels of persecution, especially under Moulay Yazid, meant that the Franciscan presence was less and less rewarding. In 1790 the Fathers left. They were to return to the city under the French Protectorate and still run a school teaching languages and career skills, besides offering such help as they can to the poor. The situation, however, is extremely precarious, as the attack on their premises and destruction of the cross outside their building in March 2010 makes clear.

**The Jewish Community at Meknès**[67]

The Jewish community in Mauretania dates back to Roman times and has survived throughout the succeeding centuries, although it suffered severe persecution under the Almohads in the 12th century. From the early 15th century, Andalusian Jews began to emigrate from Spain to North Africa. In 1438, the tensions caused by this influx combined with some obscure political scandals, led to the Jews of Fez being required to live in their own quarter, whereas previously the wealthy had lived among their Muslim counterparts and the poor among the poor. This had been the general pattern for Jewish communities in North Africa since before Islam. Segregation was a novelty and an unwelcome one.

The area to which they moved was known as the *mellah*[68] or "saline area", probably salt flats or *sebkha*, and had originally been the quarter assigned to Christian mercenaries. The word came to be used for the Jewish quarter of town throughout Morocco, although most *mellah* were only established much later, when orders were given to separate the communities in 1807. Numbers of immigrants greatly increased again after 1492 and substantial Andalusian Jewish communities were to be found in all the major cities. The second *mellah* in the country was founded at Marrakech in c.1557.

When Moulay Ismail began to build his capital at Meknès, he moved part of the Marrakech community there – they had been much persecuted under his brother Moulay Rashid. He wanted them on account of their skills as traders and bankers, the money that could be levied from them and because they had the international contacts to act as intermediaries in his dealings with foreign powers. Similarly, he actively sought to attract Jewish trading families to his dominions. His principal interest was the arms trade, since he needed modern weapons and powder for his newly formed 'Abīd guard and to fight the European enclaves that had established themselves in Morocco. The Catholic countries were, at least officially, loath to sell to him, but the English typically had no such inhibitions and it was often Jewish merchants in London or Amsterdam who arranged the transactions.

About 1682, Moulay Ismail, wanting to pull down parts of Meknès in order to extend his palace and, also for reasons of space and security, gave the Jews their own quarter in the area known today as the Old Mellah. Members of the community became his advisors, sometimes known as "Court Jews", prominent among them being Joseph Toledano. At this period, there were a number of distinguished scholars among the Jewish community at Meknès, primarily in the fields of theology and mysticism, including several members of the Toledano, Benattar and Benguigui families.[69] These names occur in Maria ter Meetelen, John Windus and other accounts of negotiations during the 18th century. In spite of some of their number holding important posts at court and frequently being extremely wealthy, the Jews were in a difficult position even under Moulay Ismail, who favoured them and, like the rest of his subjects, they were spared neither his violence nor his extortions. Captain John Braithwaite, who wrote an account of his journey with John Russell,

*Bab Mellah – entrance to the Jewish Quarter – postcard c.1900.*

the British consul, on a diplomatic mission to Fez and Meknès in 1728-9 points out:

> "...the Jews are in the greatest Fear, and pay the greatest Submission to the Moors possible, calling the meanest Moor Sir with all the forms of Respect: whereas the Moors of the meanest Quality disdain to say to the Jews any other than "Jew, do this, or Jew do that..."[70]

After the death of Moulay Ismail in 1727, the Jewish community was particularly affected by the upheavals that swept the country and the violence that shook Meknès in 1728 and again 1737. The violence at this period reflected more the breakdown of society in general than aggression aimed exclusively at the Jews, but the situation became worse towards the end of the century, especially under Moulay Yazid, whose hatred of all non-Muslims – except perhaps the English - was fanatical.

At this date, the Jews already made up a sizable minority in Meknès and by the end of the 19th century numbered 1152 families with nineteen synagogues. The community continued to grow, especially under the French protectorate, when it became necessary to build a new *mellah*.

The Jewish community lived, as Maria ter Meetelen makes clear, by trade and acting as brokers, on a very small as well as an international scale. Several accounts confirm Maria ter Meetelen's complaints that they were only interested in money and were often unreliable, but this was no doubt in part because the writers did not realize the complicated nature of the society in which they were moving, the level of the bribe culture and the fact that the rulers with whom their Jewish interfaces were attempting to negotiate changed their minds and went back on their words precisely as they pleased. Braithwaite perhaps sums up the general view:

> "There is no describing what a Set of villainous hands we got into in Mequinez : neither can I say, in that Place, which are worse, the Moors, Jews or Christians, for we found all we had to do with equally bad."[71]

### Gibraltar

Gibraltar, strategically of great importance, was bought from the Duke of Medina Sidonia by a group of Jewish *conversos* in 1474. Although they were expelled soon after, in the 18th century the town again had a strong Jewish presence. The community engaged in trade and acted as intermediaries in negotiations with North Africa. In 1704, Gibraltar was captured from the Spanish Crown by an Anglo-Dutch force and ceded "in perpetuity" to Britain in 1713. Much of the Spanish population fled back into Spain. After an unsuccessful attempt to retake Gibraltar, it was decided in 1730 to build a line of fortifications across the isthmus to prevent incursions by the British. This was completed in 1735 and the town that grew up to cater to the needs of those building and manning the wall came to be called La Línea de la Concepción. As a result of the "Gibraltar Line" and the on-going hostilities, it was essential for Britain to maintain a working relationship with some of the North African states in order to ensure the provisioning of the city and of the fleet, since this could not be done from Spain. An accommodation became increasingly important from the mid-18th century, as Gibraltar developed into one of Britain's most important naval bases. This necessity dictated Britain's policies towards the cities of the North African coast on a number of occasions and, together with the need for support in naval action against Spain, was one reason for the active diplomatic exchanges between England and Morocco from the 17th century on.

## Spain and Holland, Catholic and Protestant

Maria ter Meetelen often suggests that antagonism between Catholic and Protestant at Meknès was greater than between Christian and Muslim and it therefore seems worth saying a few words about the religious situation in the Netherlands at the time.

The original seventeen provinces that made up the Netherlands mostly came under the rule of the Holy Roman Empire at the end of the 15th century[72] and passed to Charles V in 1519 on his accession as Holy Roman Emperor. He was born in Ghent and was in many ways more Flemish than Spanish, in spite of having inherited the Spanish Empire in 1516. Nevertheless, he was a passionate Catholic and determined not to allow the political and religious dissent that was spreading across Europe, triggered, especially after 1517, by the teachings of Martin Luther, to take hold in his dominions.

In the Netherlands, therefore, Protestantism came to be associated with the Nationalist cause and the desire to expel their Spanish overlords, by whom the Dutch felt exploited financially and patronized politically. This led to the Dutch War of Independence, between the Seventeen

Provinces and Spain, which lasted from 1568 to 1648, although there were periods of truce. In 1648, the seven northern provinces became independent under the States General with, as the official faith, the Dutch Reformed Church, which had come into being about 1571. Low Church Protestant, it was politically opposed to Spain and determined to allow Catholicism no tolerance. The South of the country remained generally Catholic and under the control of Spain until 1713 when it passed to Austria.

At the time Maria ter Meetelen was writing, religious questions were still being violently debated across Europe and for someone from the Netherlands their choice of belief was of extreme importance and had far-reaching consequences in social and political, as well as spiritual, terms.

Maria ter Meetelen tells us that she was Catholic and her Reformed husband had to be persuaded to convert in order to marry her. The earlier part of her book is filled with references to the Fathers, the help they gave her, attending Mass, and so on. Later, however, these references drop away and Maria refers more often to her Bible – a marker of the Protestant as opposed to Catholic approach to Christianity. It can be imagined that, perhaps in part because of her problems with the Spanish slaves, her husband's religion reasserted itself and she in turn veered towards the Reformed Church – in any case a sensible choice, since they were going back to Medemblik in the heart of Protestant North Holland. It would also explain her son's absolute unwillingness to speak Spanish.

## Maria ter Meetelen

In the admirably researched introduction to *Christenslaven*[73], Laura van den Broek and her colleagues tell us all that can be traced of Maria ter Meetelen's life before and after her years at Meknès and it should be consulted by anyone wanting full details and sources.

Maria ter Meetelen was born in Amsterdam in 1704 to Casper ter Meetelen and Lucretia van der Heijden, a Catholic couple with numerous children. Lucretia died in childbed in 1712 and shortly after Casper remarried. In 1714, he was declared bankrupt and the financial troubles of the household, as well as, apparently, disagreements with her stepmother, probably explain why Maria ter Meetelen left home so young – although, by the standards of the time, thirteen would have been a normal age to go into service. However, she implies that her break with the family was more than simply moving to another household to work.

It is not clear what Maria ter Meetelen did over the next few years, but it is tempting to place her in the theatrical world, perhaps with a group of travelling players or musicians. It would explain her wanderings, her skill at music, her little dog – not a normal possession for a servant – her acquaintance with the Duchess of Riperda, her rather brash self-confidence, her strong sense of theatre and perhaps even her rather casual statement that she had been dressing as a man and serving as a soldier until found out.

For a woman to travel disguised as a man was a not uncommon precaution, exploited in numerous novels and plays, notably *As You Like It*. There were also a very small number of women who joined the army or navy as men and managed to carry off the deception for a surprisingly long time. However, Maria ter Meetelen does not give any suggestion she was lesbian, a habitual cross-dresser, or that she had any yearning for the military life. The impression is that it was briefly expedient and perhaps even amusing; unfortunately she gives no details. However, in order to carry off the deception even for a short while, she would surely have needed either a natural inclination or some theatrical training. It is true that she invariably presents herself as a leader: active, courageous and determined and not at all fazed by the King's gift of a weapon to defend herself, all of which lend credence to her military past.

One wonders equally about the nun's habit that she says was in her possession. It is true that she was from a Catholic family and van den Broek tells us that one of her half-sisters, Clara, became a nun in the convent at Kranenburg in Gelderland – an area where the local aristocracy protected the Catholic faith. Nevertheless, young women were not encouraged to come and go from the convent, certainly not after they had taken their vows. If Maria ter Meetelen had entered as a postulant, she would not have been wearing the full habit and would certainly not have been allowed to take it away on departure. If she were, as seems quite possible given her life, simply taking refuge in a convent, she would not have been in possession of a habit at all. Once again, the sense is much more that this was something theatrical, perhaps even mentioned for effect, rather than a serious part of her former existence. Indeed, many of her anecdotes, although they surely have a basis of truth, seem to have been given a dramatic twist with Maria ter Meetelen firmly in the starring role as heroine.

Earlier editors qualify Maria ter Meetelen's style as rough and uneducated, but today it has all the greater appeal to us for being plain and direct, close to the spoken word, so that we hear her own voice, rather than elegant set phrases. What is remarkable is that she had the self-confidence and energy – given all the problems with which she had to battle - to keep a diary during her years as a slave. Equally unusual is her careful dating of almost every event of importance. Those that can be checked are by and large correct. Her way of writing is typical of the partially educated: lively, with many colloquial expressions, long rambling sentences – stylistically normal, by the way, in the 18$^{th}$ century - a tendency to repeat words and vagueness about both pronouns and singulars and plurals. Her habit of putting herself first in any list of names may have more to do with her personality than with her literary ability. In translating, I have tried to keep some of these elements, so that her vivid, dominant, slightly coarse, but valiant and somehow engaging personality is not swamped in academic prose.

Five years after her return to Holland and retirement to her husband's town of Medemblik in North Holland, Maria ter Meetelen's book: *Wonderbaarlyke en Merkwaardinge gevallen van een twaalfjarige slaverny* was published, of which two copies survive. She did not – as one might have hoped – live happily ever after. In 1745, her husband Pieter Jansz Iede set out for the Indies – probably Batavia in the Dutch East Indies - leaving her with two children and another pregnancy that ended either in miscarriage or the early death of the child. For some reason, perhaps financial, or because of the children, she did not follow him, but in 1749 both her children died suddenly, first Frans and, two weeks later, Anna. In the following year, Pieter Jansz Iede also died, far away in the Indies. Maria ter Meetelen was left, as far as is known, alone. On the 11$^{th}$ March, 1751, she asked permission of the aldermen of Medemblik to leave for the Cape of Good Hope where, van den Broek postulates, her younger brother, Antonius may have established himself. Nothing more is recorded of her.

## Minor Characters

No information was found for several people that Maria ter Meetelen mentions, especially Dutch ship's captains, but serious research in the archives in the Netherlands might well bring more details to light.

**Louis and Francis Butler [Buttelaar],** brothers, the latter Consul of the United Provinces at Gibraltar.

**Jan Catallana** was head of all the slaves at Meknès at the time of Maria ter Meetelen's arrival.

**Jan Cornelisz Dekker**, of Zwaag in North Holland was captured off Cape St Vincent aged 14 in 1715 and remained in Morocco as a slave until the redemption of 1743.[74]

**The Guigui or Benguigui family** was important across North Africa and gave Meknès both learned rabbis and "Court Jews", among them the brothers Reuben and Eliezer Ben Guigui, sent to The Hague as ambassador in 1729 and involved on several occasions in redemptions – for example in 1730 on behalf of Ahmed ad-Dahbi - as well as negotiations in the British interest. Francis Butler reports that on November 27th, 1737 Reuben Ben Guigui together with two Dutch slaves, arrived at Tétuan.[75]

**Hendrik Lynslager** (1693-1768) was of a naval family and was sent to serve at Algiers from 1725-8. Then, during the war with Morocco, because of his experience in the region, he was involved in peace negotiations and ransoming captives. The mission, however, was unsuccessful and in 1737 he returned home. After service in Russia and the Baltic, he was sent to Algiers and Tripoli in 1750, again because of his knowledge of the area, to patrol the Straits and maintain peace. He rose through the Admiralty hierarchy to the rank of Rear Admiral in 1751. There is allegedly a half-length portrait of him in the Rijksmuseum, Amsterdam. An important cartographer, his charts were the basis for a number of very fine maps, particularly of the Straits and the Barbary Coast.[76]

**Frans van der Meer** - Ambassador at the Spanish Court, whose coachman escaped the corsairs.

**Klaas van der Meer** - Maria ter Meetelen's first husband - perhaps the Claas van der Meer who was baptized at Alkmaar on 4th October, 1691.

**William Pettycrew** – was deputy Consul at Tétuan in 1744, while Mr Latton was Consul.[77]

**The Duchess of Riperda** – Francisca Xarava del Castillo, the second wife of the Dutch adventurer Johan Willem Ripperda (1684-1737). Born a Catholic of good family, he converted to Protestantism in the interests of political advancement with the States General. In 1715 he was sent as ambassador to Spain, where he reverted to Catholicism and became Juan Guillermo, Duque de Riperdá. In 1726, guilty of large-scale misappropriation of Crown funds, he was forced to leave Spain – the French diarist Saint Simon always had doubts as to his probity. His later years are obscure. It was rumoured that he returned to Protestantism, but later found it more expedient to convert to Islam. He died at Tétuan in 1737. His daughter, Maria, by his first wife, married a Spanish nobleman and it would have been to her that Maria ter Meetelen was taking the jewels. The *Memoirs of the Duke of Ripperda*, published in 1740, claiming that he had been prime minister to Moulay Abdallah, are fascinating – but a forgery.

**Captain Joos Sels** – He was sent to Morocco to complete the peace mission begun by Captain Lager[78] and to rescue captured Dutch citizens. He reached the rank of Rear Admiral and in 1757 was sent to Algiers, again on a combined diplomatic and naval mission. His letters are apparently of considerable interest.[79]

**John Leonard Sollicoffre** was the English Consul at Tetuan at this date. On the 15th December, 1734, he signed a treaty with Moulay Abdullah, the second article of which states:

> "If any of the Emperor's subjects shall be made slaves, and shall escape to an English Man-of-War, or to Gibraltar, or to Port Mahon, or any of the English Dominions, that they shall be protected, and with all convenient speed sent to their respective homes. The like treatment to be given to the English who shall be Slaves and escape to any part of the Emperor's Dominions[80]."

Two years later, the *Calendar of Treasury Books and Papers*[81] shows for March 8th, 1736 two bills, one for £500 and one for £33 with Abraham Messias as the payee, both are entered in the King's Warrant Book as:

> "Bill drawn by John Leonard Sollicoffre late consul at Tetuan payable to Abraham Benider for value received of Bashaw Hamet Ben Ali by redemption of captive.[82]"

Sollicorffe apparently got into trouble and could not leave Morocco, because he had promised more ransom than the available funding allowed. He died on June 1st, 1735 in Tétuan. The disagreement over the ransom to be paid by England was only settled fifteen years after his death."

## The Mother of Moulay Abdallah - Sayyida Khanāta

Merely to suggest that the Mother of Moulay Abdullah was a "minor character" seems like *lèse majesté*, so the small amount of information about her given by al-Nāsirī will be found in Appendix 1 and her correspondence with the British ambassador, Charles Stewart, in Appendix 2.

# The European Slaves of North Africa in Art and Literature

The subject of European slavery aroused a good deal of interest in the 16th - 18th centuries and a surprising number of ex-slaves both Catholic and Protestant, besides Cervantes, wrote accounts of their experiences, some of which have been reprinted.[83] A selection is given in the Bibliography. There were also accounts by those involved in the redemptions, such as Father Pierre Dan, who set out in 1634 on a major ransoming mission to Algiers and wrote one of the most detailed account of the subject[84], or Diego de Haedo[85] the Younger's book, published in 1612. (This is not the place to open the fascinating debate as to whether the *Historia General de Argel* was in fact by Antonio de Sosa, a companion of Cervantes in captivity, rather than the two clerics, uncle and nephew, with the same name).[86] A number of these accounts had illustrations, usually showing the sufferings to which the slaves were subjected: those in the Dutch edition of Pierre Dan, published at Amsterdam in 1684, are particularly noteworthy, as is the frontispiece to William Okley's account,[87] but there are many others.

The innumerable paintings of slave-market and harem have already been mentioned,[88] but there are also a number of works recording the labours of the Orders, particularly from the 17th century. Among them is the famous statue by Juan de Mesa[89] of the Mercedarian, San Ramón Nonato, shown with his lips sealed with a padlock to prevent him preaching. He had offered himself in exchange for another captive whom he could not afford to ransom in the course of a 13th century redemption at Algiers. Other works include a painting of the Mercedarians, San Pietro and San Germano, paying over a ransom to an unnamed Bey, dated to c.1672. Their martyrdom is shown in the top right hand corner of the canvas.[90] The 12th century founder of the Trinitarians, San Giovanni de Matha appears in a painting by Vicente Carducho[91], in 17th century dress, presenting a letter from the Pope to the King of Morocco; while a nice drawing by Pierre Janvier, somewhat later in the century, shows a Trinitarian freeing a Christian captive[92].

# Sources

The manuscript of Maria ter Meetelen's book has long since vanished and the original edition of *Wonderbaarlyke en Merkwaardinge gevallen*

Mercedarians at Algiers Bargain with the Pacha to redeem Christian Slaves – 1662

*van een twaalfjarige slaverny*, published at Hoorn (some 20km from Medemblik) in 1748 survives in only two copies. It was reprinted by H. Harding of the Royal Archives of the Netherlands in 1950 in a work on Christian Slaves in North Africa and was then translated into French by G.H. Bousquet, the great scholar of Islamic law and especially of the Maghrib. His introduction adds a charming acknowledgement: "Lastly, I must thank my mother, who at the age of nearly seventy-five years, has not hesitated to give me the most valuable assistance thus considerably shortening my task – Kinas el-Wa'ila, October 1953 to January 1954". There was then a long hiatus, before an Arabic translation appeared, appropriately enough, in Morocco. This was followed by the excellent edition of Maria ter Meetelen, together with another longer account of slavery in North Africa, introduced by Laura van den Broek, Maaike Jacobs and G.S. van Krieken. The Bousquet version and the van den Broek edition were used in preparing this translation.

Abū Idrīs, Idrīs. *Min Tārīkh al-Maghrib wa-Hādiratihi al-ismāilīyah : Qiṣṣat al-Hūlandīyah Māriyā tīr Matalan.* Translated by Idrīs Abū Idrīs. al-Muhammadīyah: Matba'at Fadālah, 1996.

Bousquet, G-H, and G W Bousquet-Mirandolle. *L'annotation Ponctuelle De Maria Ter Meetelen.* Paris: Editions Larose, 1956.

Broek, Laura van den, Jacobs, Maaike and Krieken, G. S. van, *Christenslaven.* Zutphen: 2006.

Hardenberg, Herman. *Tussen Zeerovers en Christenslaven: Noordafrikaanse Reisjournalen.* Leiden: 1950.

One problem with a text of this kind is the transliteration of foreign words and names, particularly from Arabic. Clearly, the 17th and 18th century sources vary widely in spelling and do not use diacritical points, nor do many non-specialist modern works, such as Jamil Abun-Nasr's invaluable *History of the Maghrib*. In addition, many maps and standard sources, particularly those produced in North Africa, use French spelling for words such as Moulay or Meknès. Rationalizing all this seemed impossible and since the book is not intended for a specialist audience, I have used the most familiar forms of the names wherever possible, so that anyone who wishes can consult maps, on-line encyclopaedias or other accessible works and find what they are looking for in recognizable form. In Maria ter Meeten's own text, I have replaced Feess, for example, with Fez and Entriana with Triana, but have left some of her other orthographical eccentricities where I thought they would add flavour but not cause confusion. For Arabic names, for the reason given above, I have not used the correct academic transcription except in the Appendix, which gives extracts of a *Chronicle* translated from the Arabic, and in citations or entries from such sources as *The Encyclopaedia of Islam*. Maria ter Meetelen's text has very long paragraphs, which I have broken up for the convenience of non-specialist readers, and I have also added headings.

1  Evliya Chelebi, *Siyyah nameh*, J. von Hammer, London: 1834 pp.66, 147-8, 196, etc. and see also Halil Inalcik. "Servile Labor in the Ottoman Empire" in A. Ascher, B. K. Kiraly, and T. Halasi-Kun (eds), *The Mutual Effects of the Islamic and Judeo-Christian Worlds: The East European Pattern*, Brooklyn College, 1979, pp. 25-43.

2  Konstantin Mihailovic, *Memoirs of a Janissary*, tr.Benjamin Stolz (Ann Arbor: University of Michigan Press, 1975).

3  See also: Halil Inalcik. "Servile Labor in the Ottoman Empire" in A. Ascher, B. K. Kiraly, and T. Halasi-Kun (eds), *The Mutual Effects of the Islamic and Judeo-Christian Worlds:The East European Pattern*, Brooklyn College, 1979, pp. 25-43

4  A useful table of major raids, especially against Italy, is given in Davis, *Christian Slaves*, pp. xiv-xvi (see below).

5  Robert Davis, *Christian Slaves, Muslim Masters – White Slavery in the Mediterranean, the Barbary Coast and Italy 1500-1800* (New York: Palgrave Macmillan 2004).

6  Evliya Chelebi, *Siyyah Nameh*, Vol.II p.76

7  Miss Tully, *Letters Written During a Ten Years' Residence at the Court of Tripoli* (first published London 1816), with an Introduction by Caroline Stone. (Kilkerran: Hardinge Simpole 2009), p 81-2

8  Elizabeth Marsh, *The Female Captive*, (originally published under the name Mrs Crisp, London 1769) ed. Khalid Bekkaoui, (Casablanca: 2003); Linda Colley, *The Ordeal of Elizabeth Marsh* (London: Harper, 2007).

9  A reference to the famous story, told in Christopher Marlowe's *Tamburlane*, that when in 1402 Tamburlane (Timur) captured the Ottoman Sultan Bayezid I at the battle of Ankara, he imprisoned him in a cage and Bayezid killed himself by dashing his brains out against the bars.

10  William Oakely, *A Small Monument of Great Mercy*, (London: 1675; this ed.1764) pp. 26- 27.

11  Oakely, *A Small Monument* , p.8

12  *The Diary of Samuel Pepys*, 8th February, 1661 and on-line at www.pepysdiary.com

13  *The Tangier Papers of Samuel Pepys*, ed. Edwin Chappell, Printed for the Naval Records Office, (London: 1935), p.288.
14  Nicholas Harding, "North African Piracy, the Hannoverian Carrying Trade and the British State 1728-1828," *The Historical Journal* 43, no. 1 (2000).
15  John Windus, *A Journey to Mequinez*. (London: 1725) – and many other examples
16  At this date the Catalans were carving out possessions across the eastern Mediterranean – and like the Venetians and Genoese were involved in the slave trade.
17  *Chansons Populaires Grecques des XV et XVI siècles*, ed. Hubert Pernod, (Paris: 1931) p.85
18  Jarbel Rodriguez, *Captives and Their Saviors in the Medieval Crown of Aragon* (Washington D.C.: The Catholic University of America Press, 2007).
19  Rodriguez, *Captives*, p.206.
20  Rodriguez, *Captives*, p.135; Andrés Díaz Borrás, *El miedo al Mediterranáneo: La caridad popular valenciana y la redención de cautivos bajo poder Musulmán, 1323-1539* (Barcelona: 2001).
21  Rodriguez, *Captives*, p.156
22  Rodriguez, *Captives*, p.182
23  Long term converts and those perceived as real apostates were, of course, not eligible for ransom.
24  New Advent, *Order of Trinitarians, Order of Our Lady of Mercy - Mercedarians* www.newadvent.org
25  See *Jewish Encyclopaedia* under Captives, Slaves, *Parnas*, etc. also on-line at www.jewishencyclopaedia.com
26  Miss Tully, *Letters*, pp.65-73
27  John Braithwaite, *The History of the Revolutions...In the Empire of Morocco* (London: 1729).
28  J. Buchan Telfer, *The Bondage and Travels of Johann Schiltberger* (London: Hakluyt Society, 1879)
29  Miguel de Cervantes, *Trato de Argel*, from "Segunda jornada" lines 870-1035. *Los Baños de Argel and La Gran Sultana* also based on this period of his life, as are episodes in *Don Quixote* and his other writings.
30  María Antonia Garcés, *Cervantes in Algiers: A Captive's Tale* (Nashville: Vanderbilt University Press, 2002).
31  Miss Tully, *Letters*, p.206.
32  Roger Perkins and Captain K.J.Douglas-Morris, *Gunfire in Barbary*, (London: 1982), pp.22-3.
33  Bernard Lewis, "Corsairs in Iceland," *Revue de l'Occident Musulman et le Méditerranée* 15, 1973 and on-line at www.persee.fr.
34  Jane Lyons, The Baltimore Raid, www.from-ireland.net/history and on Jan Jansen; Francis Ferraro,    Anthony Jansen van Salee www.

genforum.genealogy.com. Des Ekin, *The Stolen Village: Baltimore and the Barbary Pirates* (Dublin: 2008).

35 In other words, his conversion had been ratified by a local *marabout* or holy man and he had been dressed in local dress to symbolize his moving from the Christian to the Muslim world.
36 Braithwaite, *The History of the Revolutions...In the Empire of Morocco*.
37 Braithwaite, *The History*, p.133.
38 "Vasallos libres de la Corona" – concern had arisen much earlier and legal action designed to protect the Indians is found in the *Leyes de Burgos* of 1512
39 E(lizabeth)(M)arsh, *The Female Captive*, London: 1769, edited by Khalid Bekkaoui, Casablanca: Moroccan Cultural Studies, 2003 and also Linda Colley, *The Ordeal of Elizabeth Marsh* (New York: Pantheon, 2007).
40 An interesting insight into the Muslim views of slavery is to be found in Ahmad Shafiq, *L'esclave Du Point De Vue Musulman* (Cairo: 1892; reprint, Cornell U.P.).
41 Cevdat Pasha, *Tezakir* 1-12, Ankara: 1953 pp.101-152 for detailed account and full documentation, quoted in Bernard Lewis *Race and Slavery* (Oxford: 1990), p81
42 James Richardson, *Travels in Morocco*, London c.1857 published posthumously, Vol.I ch.7
43 Although the context was somewhat different, the patriotic song, *Rule Britannia* dating from 1740, expressed this sentiment in the refrain: "Britons never will be slaves!"
44 Lynne Thornton, *Women as Portrayed in Orientalist Painting* (Paris: ACR, 1994).
45 Florence MacAlistair, *Memoir of Sir John McNeill*.....London: 1910 quoted in Katie Hickman, *Daughters of Britannia*, London: 1999 p.241
46 Pat Shipman, The *Stolen Woman*, London: 2004 and Samuel Baker, *Ismailia* (London: 1874), the latter forthcoming in this series
47 Pietro della Valle, *I Viaggi Di Pietro Della Valle (c.1616-1623)*, Il Nuovo Ramusio. (Rome: Istituto Poligrafico dello Stato, 1972).
48 Jamil Abun-Nasr, *A History of the Maghrib in the Islamic Period* (Cambridge: Cambridge U.P., 1987).
49 Abun-Nasr, pp. 119-224
50 Abul Nasir Mulay Ismail as-Samin bin Sharif
51 Sala Colonia
52 Braithwaite, *The History of the Revolutions*, pp.190-1
53 Patricia Crone, *Slaves on Horses: The Evolution of the Islamic Polity* (Cambridge: Cambridge University Press, 1980).
54 Daniel Pipes, *Slave Soldiers and Islam: The Genesis of a Military System* (Chicago: 1981).
55 E of I article *Miknās al-Zaytūn*

56  Windus, *A Journey*, p.115. The distance is in the order of 54 km or 35 miles.
57  Much of the information in this section is taken from Henri Koehler, *L'eglise Chrétienne Du Maroc Et La Mission Franciscaine 1221-1790* (Paris: 1934)
58  Henri Koehler, *L'eglise Chrétienne*.
59  Windus, *A Journey*, p.155
60  Henri Koehler, *L'eglise Chrétienne, passim*.
61  Windus, *A Journey*, pp.195-6
62  *Christenslaven*, p.337
63  Koehler, *L'eglise Chrétienne*, pp.157-8
64  Rodriguez, *Captives*, p.37 et seq.
65  Koehler, *L'eglise Chrétienne*, pp.161
66  P.-L. Blanc, "Earthquakes and Tsunami in November 1755 in Morocco: A Different Reading of Contemporaneous Documentary Sources," *Natural Hazards and Earth System Sciences / Institut de Radioprotection et de Sûreté Nucléaire* (2009).
67  For an in-depth descripton, see: Haim Zeer Hirschberg and et al., *A History of the Jews in North Africa: From the Ottoman Conquests to the Present Time* (Leiden: Brill, 1981).
68  See E of I article *Mallāh*
69  Joseph Tolédano, *Le Temps Du Mellah* (Jerusalem: 1982). p.90.
70  Braithwaite, *The History*, p.115
71  Braithwaite, *The History*, p.216-7
72  About 1482.
73  Laura van den Broek, *Christenslaven* (Zutphen: 2006).
74  See www.turksmuseum.nl and Joos Vermeulen, *Sultans, slaven en renegaten*, (Leuven: 2001), p.220
75  Joseph Tolédano, *Le Temps du Mellah*, p.79 et seq.; L van der B n. 172 and n.177.
76  See his map of the Straits of Gibraltar plate no. 23 in the 1747 issue of Ratelband's "Geographisch-Toneel", 1693-1768; also *Nieuwe Paskaart von't Naauw van de Straat... door H. Lynslager. Uytgegeven by A. en H. de Leth ... 1726.-- Amsterdam, 1727*. Also the Nederlands Dictionary of National Biography at www.biografischportaal.nl
77  See the *Calendar of Treasury Books and Papers* vol.5 ed. William A. Shaw and *Treasury Minutes* book XXX pp.7-10 on-line at www.british-history.ac.uk
78  sic – but could this be Captain Lynslager?
79  Alexander H. de Groot, *Ottoman North Africa and the Dutch Republic in the seventeenth and eighteenth century* in Revue de l'Occident Musulman et de la Méditerranée, 1985, vol.39, pp. 131-147 and on-line at www.persee.fr and Nederlands D.N.B.

80  *British and Foreign State Papers* vol.I part 1, p.432, Foreign Office, London 1841
81  Vol III 1735-8 ed. William A. Shaw, London, 1900, p.179
82  Also on-line at www.british-history.ac.uk
83  For example: Daniel J. Vitkus, *Piracy, Slavery and Redemption: Barbary Captivity Narratives from Early Modern England (16th-18th Centuries)* (New York: Columbia University Press, 2001).
84  Pierre Dan, *Histoire De Barbarie Et Ses Corsaires* (Paris: 1612)
85  Diego de Haedo, *Topographía E Historia General De Argel*. (Valladolid: 1612)
86  Garcés, *Cervantes in Algiers: A Captive's Tale*.
87  William Okley, *Eben-Ezer, or a Small Monument of Great Mercy* (London: 1674).
88  Thornton, *Women as Portrayed in Orientalist Painting*.
89  In the Museo de las Bellas Artes in Seville, originally the Mercedarian Convent.
90  In the sacristy of the Church of Nostra Signora di Bonaria, Cagliari, see Giancarlo Rocca, "La Sostanza Dell'effimero: Gli Abiti Degli Ordini Religiosi in Occidente," ed. Museo Nazionale di Castel Sant' Angelo (Roma: Edizioni Paoline, 2000).
91  Museo del Prado, Madrid
92  From Fastes et annales des évêques de Meaux, Meaux, France; Médiathèque Luxembourg ms.79.

# Maria ter Meetelen

**The Wanderings of a Transvestite**

The way things happen in this world is extraordinary and I am going to tell the reader something about my own destiny.

From the age of thirteen I wandered abroad and at twenty-one I decided to take a little trip across France dressed as a man. In this way, I arrived in Spain at a town called Vitoria[1] where I was forced by the press gang into a Frisian Dragoon Regiment. I did not stay long, for they soon discovered that I was not the person under whose name I was registered. I went back to women's clothes and set out for Madrid with the wife of the standard-bearer. After having remained there for a while, at last I married a Dutch captain from Alkmaar, called Klaas van der Meer[2], on October 22nd, 1728.

At that time, I was about twenty-four years old. My husband, who was involved in a lawsuit because his boat had been confiscated, was obliged to put off our departure, which finally took place on the 15th of January, 1731. We arrived on the 22nd of that month at Carmona[3], which is less than a day's journey from Seville. Then we rented another house in Triana[4] facing Seville and stayed there until the 27th of June when we requested a passport for Holland, which we obtained through the Ambassador of the High Powers[5] and the Prime Minister of his Royal Majesty.

Seeing that the business went on and on, we went to Sanlúcar de Barrameda[6], two miles from Seville, where, on the 7th of July in the year 1731 we embarked in a *buys*[7] and set out to sea in her on the 8th. We arrived in sight of Cape St Vincent, where we saw a boat we thought was Turkish[8]. My husband suggested that the captain should load his guns and his artillery, which consisted of three three-pounders and two little *basjes*[9]. Fortified positions too were set up, as if in preparation for a battle. However, the wind turned and we went back more than we went forward, so that we were forced to leave the Portuguese coast sideways and head for the open sea. The wind grew stronger, it rained and that evening we had very bad weather so that we had to strike sail.

## Corsairs

My husband was made very gloomy by these events and he wished many times that the topmast would fall so we would be forced to head for Cape St Vincent. In that case we would have landed and gone on to Holland overland, for the idea that the ship was going to be captured was firmly anchored in his head. Then the wind changed again and we headed for Holland and thus on Saturday, July 21$^{st}$ we arrived near Barles[10] at the level of the 22$^{nd}$ mile. It was completely calm and custom required that anyone who had never been through Barles should be baptized. Now, I had never yet been through, so my little dog and I were obliged to be baptized. So, I offered a vat of wine[11] for myself and two *rijksdaalders*[12] for my dog, with the result that the crew was put in a cheerful mood.

So, it was about midday when the helmsman had gone off duty and, as usual, a man then went up the mast to see if there were any ships in the neighbourhood. So, someone had gone up, but had not seen any ship. During this time, the captain and the helmsman had gone down to the cabin. I happened to be on the big hatch and there was a man at the helm. Now, another one came to steer, who snatched his - the first man's - shirt off, tore it to shreds and threw it over the side. I watched this and was absolutely staggered. I thought at once of the Turks, who would steal our clothes like that. At just that moment the kitchen boy came up from storeroom. He had finished washing up and stood by the tiller, looked at the sea and saw two ships. At once, he called out to me:

"Miss, miss, there's a ship!"

I got up at once to look. Instead of one, we saw two. We could hardly see what kind of ships they were. My heart stopped, for it was as if I could already see that it was a Turk. My husband went to warn the captain and the helmsman who arrived at once with the telescope. As it was absolutely calm, we were hardly moving. They could see that it was not a friendly ship and there had been fighting, which was confirmed when they drew near us. The Turk must have received some hard blows from a French ship he had thought to overcome, but the fox had been too cunning for him, and as soon as he saw us, he left the French ship.

It was about four in the afternoon when they saw us. They hailed us, telling us to come along side in our dinghy with our passport. Our captain signalled to them to find out where they were from. They said Algiers and, as there were so many whites on board, we thought it was from Algiers, but still we doubted somewhat. Our men set about launching the rowing boat, while the captain hunted through his papers, but they were already so distressed and demoralized that they did not know how to launch it fast enough, so they took a knife and cut the ropes.

## The Crew Flees

Meanwhile, the captain had decided to defend himself and so he had the cannons and guns got ready and great preparations were made for battle. The crew didn't seem to have much appetite for it. They lowered the rowing boat and put three muskets and some powder in it in order to flee. The boat was in no state to defend itself against a Turk with 20 pieces of ordinance and 150 men, for we were only eleven souls, six men, a cabin boy and four passengers.

My husband, seeing that they were going to flee, pressed me to get into the rowing boat as well. I did not want to agree to it, or else he was to come with me, but he had lost his head so completely that he did not know what he should or should not do. He answered that he had no right to abandon the ship, but that I had to leave; however, I said that I didn't want that. If he was made captive, I wanted to be taken too and then we would be together. He told me that in slavery it would be impossible to stay together – that one of us would be sold here, the other there. That still didn't convince me to get into the rowing boat. The proverb that says:

"When God wants to punish a country, He takes all wisdom from its leaders" is not a vain one; anyway, it was certainly true in our case.

The rowing boat pulled away from the ship and it was agreed that we would give a signal if this were not enemy shipping. There were seven men in the rowing boat: the helmsman, the cooks and three sailors and the coachman of His Excellency van der Meer[13], who was a passenger.

The Turk, seeing this, thought that the rowing boat was heading towards them. But as soon as he saw that it was fleeing, he lowered his longboat with some twenty men with guns, but they didn't manage to get under weigh fast, which was very much to the rowing boat's advantage, for they were able to escape quickly before the longboat could leave the side of the Turkish ship. The longboat had barely set out when the Turk forced us to lower the sails and flag by threatening to fire on us.

## The Corsairs Attack

My husband and the captain stood by the main sail to lower it and I stood behind next to the flag, which I lowered. I thought: better that than to be shot at because in fact it was completely impossible for us to defend ourselves. As soon as the sails and flag were struck, the Turks approached to storm the ship. My husband immediately sent me to the cabin. I took my little dog in my arms and lay down on the lower bunk and closed it. I held the sliding door with one hand and with the other I held the little dog's muzzle shut. I had hardly settled there when the Turks were already on board and they tore off my husband's and the captain's and the other passengers' clothes. Then a black came into the cabin, which he completely looted. When they had stolen everything, they banged on the sliding door of the lower bunk to search further, but I held it so firmly that it wouldn't open.

I had left a little gap in the sliding door through which I could see, and I noted everything the black man was doing. No one but this black entered and I heard nothing more of the Christians. So, I thought they were all dead. I decided I would die there in the lower bunk, if only I could get rid of the dog. But I couldn't see how to do it without being discovered. I was not afraid of being killed by them, but what I feared above all was that they would rape me. I much preferred dying to falling into their hands. That is why I took the decision to stay in the lower bunk until my death.

After spending an hour there, more or less, I heard my husband calling me. When I heard his voice, I gave a cry, leapt from the bunk and rushed on to the deck. My husband, astonished at such a cry, asked if they had hurt me. I said no, because none of the Moors[14] had yet seen me, which astonished them - the Moors - very much because they did not know where I had come from. They went straight down to the cabin to see where I had been and found the place and the little dog and some valuable things and a little money and a box with some jewels to wear around the neck and the head and the diamond necklace which had been entrusted to me by the Duchess of Riperda[15] for her husband's daughter, because she trusted me, and me alone, to get them to her, since her stepdaughter and I were close friends.

The Moors took all this. So I went up on the deck where I found my husband, the captain and a passenger, who had been pastry cook to the King of Spain, and tears were streaming down the cheeks of all three of them. They stood there like criminals condemned to death with their clothes that the Moors had torn. Immediately, the Moors came over to stare at me. I took one look at this great mass of men and went to the rear next to the helm. There was a great chest there, which had held the porcelain that the captain had taken to Spain and in which I had put my winter clothes, spare linen and sweetmeats that would not fit in my trunks. A Moor was sitting on it; he had claimed it for himself. I made him get up and took out what I needed, after which I had the Moor sit back down on it. I told him to guard it and said I would give him something. I had got out a cake with candied fruit and gave him a piece, then I went back to my companions whom I comforted as best I could.

**The Ship is Looted**

Personally, I felt no great grief and did not shed a tear. I proceeded to fall into conversation with these people as if they were not enemies. I saw that they were bringing up from the hold my trunks, where I had packed my clothes, and were destroying them by hitting them. I gave them the keys so that they could open them easily but they did not have the patience. Then they took my damask dresses and knotted them over their bare skin, covering their own clothes and they did the same with all my things until they had emptied my trunks. I watched all this with dry eyes and I thought:

"God gave it to me and God has taken it from me, blessed is the name of Lord."

I had among other things two Spanish wineskins made of leather with some wine and at the top there were wooden spouts so that one only had to put them to one's mouth in order to drink. I saw that the Moors had them and were drinking. At once I went over to them and took them away from them and I brought them to my companions and encouraged them a little. I would have liked them to take the affair as lightly as I did, but it was in vain; I could not be grief-stricken for I counted myself very lucky to have kept my husband. My husband made my heart somewhat heavy by telling me that once we arrived in the land of the Turks we would be sold, going our separate ways, so we would be parted and never see each other again; but I could not believe it. I did not want to make myself miserable in advance, as I told him.

That evening, after sunset, the longboat, which had been on the heels of our rowing boat, so close that they knew how many people were in her, came back. They immediately put the captain on board and I greeted him with a fine compliment in Spanish that he, as well as some of his men, could understand. I begged him to give me back a few of my clothes and he at once promised to do what he could to retrieve some dresses and give them to me, which in fact he later did. These people then turned over to him all the gold, silver, money and other jewels, except for the clothes, which they kept for themselves. Then they took us in their longboat and led us on board their ship. Having got there, they questioned me as to the contents of our boat, of which they took note, and promised me that we could go back on board our ship and they would just check whether our passports were in order. He kept on saying:

"Flamingo[16], good passports, tomorrow you can go."

But I was well aware that he was mocking us. Then he gave me a small leather bag containing dates, raisins, figs and a little of his better ships' biscuit to eat, but none of us felt like eating, except for me.

Next, they took us under the deck, where the officers were lodged. There, they gave me some bedding and my companions got a carpet and some mats to sleep on. That night we had the most terrible weather, with thunder and heavy rain. We thought we would drown that night, for we were swimming in water. The Moors did nothing but man the pumps and call on their Magome [Muhammad]. There was little sleep that night and it was only towards dawn that I rested a little.

I think it was about 10 o'clock when I woke up. I looked around me a little and then went up on the bridge where I saw the Moors strutting about dressed in all my lovely clothes, my aprons[17] of flowered calico and my embroidered ones wrapped round the heads of these really black men. They were dancing and singing with pleasure and making a lot of noise. Others had put on my gowns and were dancing in them until at last they succeeded in tearing them to pieces and they threw the stays overboard. I had already been watching this scene for quite a while when I was overcome with sadness and cried bitterly. My husband was so strongly affected that I thought he was going to give up the ghost. He tried to comfort me in so far as possible, but he had a real need of being comforted himself.

I thought all this over in private and considered repeatedly that I was not going to gain anything by letting myself give in to this grief, but only harm body and soul. So, I calmed my heart and as long as I remained on the corsairs' boat I distracted myself by playing my zither and singing. The captain paid much attention to me and had me brought everything I wanted and he came to see me four or five times a day to find out whether I needed anything. I refused nothing, given that my husband and the other people did not get much, so at night I would take them what I had been given during the day and they ate it. Sometimes in the daytime the captain sent a black with his instrument and every evening to amuse me a little we would play, seeing who could outdo the other, each on his instrument. And we sang, I in Spanish and he in Turkish, right up to the moment that we arrived at Salé, which was on the last day of July. He had me come to his cabin and showed me the clothes he had bought back[18] for me for 32 *rijksdaalders*. He did not want to give them to me as yet for fear that the crew would seize them again, but he would give them to me when we went before the King.

**Arrival at Meknès**

On the last evening in July we came to Salé to the house of the Governor, where the merchants came to visit us and asked me what was my religion. I said Reformed, but my husband said nothing, which annoyed me, since we were in another land where there was no fear about religion[19]. But he did so because the merchants were all Catholics and we were in slavery, and because I came from Catholic parents, it couldn't be kept a secret that I was Catholic, so that he would be the one to suffer if it looked as if he had enticed me away me away from my faith. And on the other hand I still had the skirt of the habit that I had put on in 1727, which would also betray me, so that it was impossible it wouldn't come out.

During our stay in Salé, we were relatively well off and did not suffer privations. We were there until the 10th August when I went in the morning to the captain, who gave me a great bag of clothes, a woollen mattress, a quilted coverlet and a quarter[20] cask of red wine, a pair of earrings, a cross with fake stones and various other trinkets. Then, they took me to the town of Meknès[21], where we arrived on the 12th of the same month, towards evening and the head[22] of the Dutch community came to us. I was then very ill at ease. We were taken to a Moorish house where we were supposed to stay as long as we had not been before the King and that lasted at least some four days.

I was then very ill and the Fathers[23] who lived there came to visit me with their doctor and at once got me everything I needed. They showed me the most overwhelming friendship, because I was of their religion. They arranged things, through interceding with the Bashi[24], so that on the following day I could move into the house of a Spanish woman with her husband and children, and the head of the Dutch community[25] and another Dutch slave took me there. Furthermore, my husband said:

"Ah! Well, Mie, is the dream that you dreamed coming to pass, the one that I have forgotten?"

*Bab Mansour– postcard c.1910.*

But it was as if I would marry this head of the community, as indeed happened later. I was ill then and my husband in good health, but he entrusted me to this head. He said:

"Fellow countryman, I am going to die; look after my wife, she will be a good wife for you."

But the head replied:

"Oh, my fellow countryman, you should not speak like this. We will soon be set free and we will cross North Holland in a carriage, you with your little wife and me with some girl."

But it was no good. He would not let go of the idea that he was going to die.

## Brought Before the King – Moulay Abdallah

So I arrived at the Spanish house and I was well received there. I immediately had the use of a room with a bed and the food I needed. We still had to appear before the King and we were led there on the 17th of the month. I was already somewhat better and my husband was ill, so that it was very difficult for him to go to the King. Before we went to the King, the captain gave me, among other things, some of my silver and gold jewellery, as well as a ring with a ruby and two diamonds, and some hairpins and brooches with gems, for he thought that the King would keep me with him and that I would enjoy favour with the King and then I would recommend him to the King. I was young and not ugly and seemed younger than my age, for the head of the [Dutch] community took me for a young girl of 14, although I was already 27, for he said to my husband:

"Who is this young girl?"

And when my husband said that I was his wife, he found it very surprising.

So we came before the King who questioned us and handed us – my husband and me - over to this Spaniard and said that he should take care of us. In this way my husband and I were dispensed from royal service[26]. But my captain and the passenger had to set to work at once. Nevertheless, I was taken before the Bashi and I had to enumerate all the things the boat had contained and, to the great relief of the captain, I omitted to mention some of them. After having made my report, I begged the Bashi to let the captain go free and I obtained what I asked. But it only lasted a short while, 14 days, so that the Bashi did not altogether keep his word.

## The Death of Maria's Husband

My husband's illness got worse from day to day, so that I was expecting nothing but death. He then wanted with all his might to be in the monastery; he was sure he would be better there, and the Spaniard helped him, but with great difficulty, given that no-one enters there unless they are Spanish or unless they are Catholic. And, as my husband was Reformed, that caused difficulties. They put up with the situation, hoping for the opportunity to win a soul and therefore accepted him at the monastery, where he died on the ninth day. Meanwhile, I remained at the house and went to visit my husband, roughly every two days, when I was given permission. The mother of the Spanish woman also lived in that house with her and I talked to her every day about the adventures she had had while in slavery, for she was already in that state as a child of eight, as well as three of her sisters, two of whom had become wives of the King. And [I heard] everything she had had to endure: one of her children turned Turk[27] and another burned alive; how she had been forced to marry against her will on the orders of the King and plenty of other similar things. I listened very carefully to this account and learned from it, for later I could make use of it.

So, on the 8th of September, I came to the monastery very early in the morning to hear Mass and on going into my husband's room, I found him like one dead. I covered him up again, because on account of the darkness I could not see what the matter was; he did not say a word. Then I went to the church, very sad, because I could not do otherwise. Little by little, dawn broke and when it [Mass] was over I went back to my husband and nursed him with warm covers and hot stones. The doctor administered a cordial, which revived him a little and he began to speak and enjoined the Fathers to write his will[28], which he signed with the greatest difficulty and he named as his witnesses the captain and the head [of the Dutch community] and they signed this same document, which I can still show today. The Fathers worked hard trying to convert my husband to the Roman Catholic religion. Meanwhile, I comforted my husband as best I could, I prayed for him and encouraged him saying that he only had to place his confidence solely in the merits of Christ, out Redeemer. And that we should come to bliss by His grace and that Christ alone through grace could wash away our sins. I read him the Ten Commandments, the Symbol of the Christians[29], the Our Father, Psalm 51[30] and other prayers relating to the Passion of Christ and these he repeated as long as he could speak.

My husband then remained for a good two hours with his eyes closed and then at last he opened them with such a terrible expression that I fled from the room. Then he was like death itself. I will never forget that sudden change of colour. So I went back in as he was giving up his last breath. I was all alone and had spent the whole day alone with him, but the sadness that overwhelmed my soul was great, considering that I found myself in a country where I was a stranger and a slave and no longer master of myself and I was in danger of the King luring me to him. I then begged the Christians to bury the corpse.

**Choosing a New Husband**

After which I went back to the house and considered what I had better do. I prayed God to grant me what would be best for me and save me. I was very afraid of the foreign nationals because of their wealth and they could demand that the King hand me over to them through the power of their money and indeed afterwards there were three who demanded to have me, but I took a quick resolution to make the choice myself with the help of the Fathers who were there. I would pray them to lend a hand and help me in everything.

But in this, there was a great difficulty, because there was not a single Catholic in the Dutch community and for that reason it was very hard to make a choice within that nation, unless one of them wanted to become Catholic, for in that case the Fathers would pursue the matter with even more zeal. I thought:

"Here, one mustn't wait, but make a quick choice, before the King gives me to some foreign national."

On the 9th of September, in the afternoon, I therefore took the decision of choosing the head of the Dutch community, for he seemed to me the most respectable of all the Dutchmen, as indeed I was able to establish later. Fate decreed that the Fathers came to visit me that afternoon to console me for the loss of my husband. And they brought me some things that the merchants of Salé had kept for me and which they had sent to the Fathers. I took advantage of the occasion to beg the Fathers to authorize me to come on the following day to their monastery, and I prayed them to advise me in everything and to help me. They agreed to this with great approbation and promised to lend me a hand in so far as possible, which greatly comforted me.

So, in the morning, on the 10th of that same month, I went in to the cloister and told the Father Superior of my plan, which he thoroughly approved. The person I wanted to marry was an excellent man, esteemed by all the Christians and especially by them [the Fathers], but he was of another religion and that was the obstacle, otherwise he would have to change his beliefs; in that case, they would help me in every possible way. Now there was there another Father, who got up and said:

"Oh, Pieter the Fleming is a good chap, he will surely change."

I thought – that would really suit me down to the ground; it's going to work. The Fathers then promised that they would have the head [of the Dutch community] come to them and see whether they could persuade him to become Catholic. Then I went back to the house; I hadn't yet spoken to the head, so I did not know whether he would take the matter well or badly. That same afternoon, he came to me and we discussed the subject. He had already been to the Fathers and after that he came to see me. He was somewhat opposed to this affair, but at the same time wanted to accept, but not to change religion.

After spending a long time weighing the pros and cons, he finally decided to change his beliefs and thus marry me, for there was no other solution. I was delighted. We exchanged marriage vows and the next day went to the Fathers who were just as happy as if they had received a gift of a hundred thousand *rijksdaalders*. They then took endless pains with the Bashi and the leaders attached to the King, to beseech the King to give permission for this marriage and bring it to a conclusion, for over there it is in fact impossible for Christians to marry unless the King gives them to each other, since we were all, males and females, slaves of the King.

Then I went home much calmed in the hope that the Fathers would arrange everything, given that they were well seen by the King and his Grandees. Meanwhile, finding myself back at the house of the woman of whom I have spoken and telling her about the affair, they were much displeased. The man of the house was called Jan Catallana[31] and everyday he was at the Court of the King distributing and collecting up the soldiers' guns and watching over the King's warehouses[32] with some other Christians. He came home that evening and said that there were three Christians who were asking the King for me and they had plenty of money. In this, he thought he was doing me a great service, but I immediately retorted that I preferred a Dutchman in nothing but his shirt to a Spaniard or a Frenchmen with a princely fortune. He was terribly angry, but he still did not know what point my affairs had reached. But as soon as he had learned of it through his wife and the mother of his wife, I was insulted in a way most terrible to hear and they even spat in my face with rage. I kept quiet and let them go on until they were tired, after which they tried to persuade me with sweet words to accept the situation and they offered me the brother of his wife, a lad of fourteen and monstrously fat. But I would not give in, so it was all in vain.

When they saw that I held to my own countrymen, they dreamed up something else. Among the Dutch nationals, there was a Jew who lived in the house of a Bashi and also had the right to keep a tavern and so had cash. They wanted to pair me up with this Jew and threatened me with the Bashi. If he would only give him a silk belt and a little money as a gift, he could have me.

He brought me the Jew, who told me what has just been said, i.e. that he had enough money and if it was a matter of money, he would have plenty of friends who would provide him with an *allemout*, which is to say a *tak*[33], and plenty more besides. I said that I would rather die than take anyone other than the one I had already chosen. They threatened me in all sorts of ways, but I did not give in, but everyday I had to put up with insults and humiliations. In the meantime, the headman had to endure plenty of reproaches, insults and mockery. We could not visit each other every day as we would have wished, to tell of our adventures; we had to swallow it all down without saying a word.

**Audience with the King**

The Fathers, however, had already managed to present my case to the King, who summoned me early in the morning of the 17th September. Then, the woman of the house made me take off my clothes right down to my underwear. She had me put on some old rags of hers and a tattered diaper on my head, with bits of it floating round my head and my hair coming out through the holes. She did this so that I would appear at my worst before the King, since I was young and beautiful, according to the taste of the people of this country. I took my zither and my little dog and thus went to the royal house. I had Jan Corneliszoon Dekker from Swaag[34] to take me to the Royal Court. As soon as I arrived, I came across Jan Catallana who told me first that he had talked with the King, who had told him that if I took a Christian other than the Jew [sic] who was his Christian, the King would have me put to death. I replied that the King could do what he wanted for I would not accept as my husband any Christian other than the leader of the Dutch community.

"Well," he said, "do you prefer death to obeying the will of the King?"

Yes, I said, at which point a capon[35] came to fetch me at once and I was led before the King. So I found myself before the King in his chamber where he was lying and there were at least 50 women, one more beautiful than the next, their faces painted, dressed like goddesses, extraordinarily beautiful and each with the instrument on which they played and sang, and the melody was so splendid, that I have never heard anything like it. Four of the principal wives of the King were sitting facing him, shining with gold and silver and real pearls, which hung round their necks weighing pounds and on their heads, precious stones and crowns of gold and pearls, their fingers were covered with gold rings and their arms were full of bracelets of gold and silver, and their legs had circles of gold[36] each weighing several pounds at least. And the jewels round their necks hung down to their stomachs so that I asked myself how they could hold their heads up straight with all this gold and pearls and precious stones. Gold rings were plaited into their hair interspersed with gold ducats.

The King was resting his head on the knees of one of the women, his feet on the knees of another and one behind him and another in front were caressing him. They were also splendidly dressed, but not as much as the others. So, I presented myself before all this wealth like a beggar, or worse. At once, the King had the music stop and had me approach and sit down and made me play my zither. I did not understand a word the King said, but only the gestures he made. I played for a good hour before the King, which pleased him; he spoke to me, but I couldn't understand. But at last I understood what he wanted to know: whether I was French or Spanish or Dutch or English, from which nation; and whether I would turn Turk, after which I would be his wife. I could not answer him because I did not know what he was saying.

After I had been with him a good hour, a woman came and made me leave the King, after she had spoken for a minute with the King who ordered her to make me a Turk and when this was done, she was to dress me in the most beautiful way and then she would bring me back to the King. This woman did nothing except dress young virgins for the King, because he had to have a virgin every Friday. Furthermore, he had summoned all the other women of whom he had previously made use. He did not approach those who were pregnant, because it is a sin to have relations with a woman who has already been impregnated.

## The King's Women Try to Force Maria to Convert[37]

This woman took me by the hand and led me along several dark corridors in the palace until we got to another place where I found four more women or young virgins and I was added to their number. Among them was the daughter of a renegade who knew a little bad Spanish and told me that the King had ordered her to make me turn Turk. Then, I would be dressed as splendidly as the other four women seated by the King and then I would become the King's intended. Otherwise, the King would have me burned and the flesh torn from my body with pincers and I would be made to die by all sorts of tortures. I didn't understand any of this, but they made signs to me. I answered and made signs that I would rather die than be a Turk. When they understood this of me, they spat on me and hit me and abused me. After this, they came back again with flattery and sweet words and dressed me in their beautiful clothes and put a crown on my head and made signs that I would be dressed even more richly by the King and they stood before me with their fingers spread out and said: "*Chet*"[38], which means: "Believe in Magomet [Muhammad]." But when I refused, they snatched the clothes off me again and spat and cursed me yet once more. I was not a little intimidated, but I sought consolation in God. I could not go so far as to offer a prayer to God, but I put myself under His Holy Protection. I had good hope that God would well and truly help me.

At this point, he [sic] came with food for them from the King and so they separated from me and sat down in a great room to eat. They wanted me to join them, but I refused to go with them and so I stayed alone in that place, which gave me the opportunity of addressing my prayer to God. Then I fell on my knees with my face raised to heaven and prayed passionately to God with tears running down my cheeks. I begged Him to give me strength and to uphold me by His Holy Spirit so as to face the most terrible of deaths rather than deny my faith. I did not make a long prayer, but a short one and during this prayer I felt myself relieved, for the fear of death left me. Then I became bold and much preferred to die rather than give up my beliefs, considering all riches as smoke that vanishes away, and I turned from it in disgust and I had a great desire to give myself up to death as a martyr for the faith of Our Lord Jesus Christ. I was so happy in my soul that I cannot describe it; in any case the joy was a thousand times greater than the anguish I had experienced before.

After the women had eaten, they came back to me, to persuade me to

*Ruins of the Dar al-Makhzen – photograph: R. Gréberl, c.1900.*

become a Moor, but I was much more insolent. I pushed them away from me and signed to them that they could just cut my throat; that I preferred to die rather than turn Turk. They were quite astonished that I dared to push them away so audaciously; they insulted me enthusiastically and spat on me. I began to feel ill, because I had not yet had anything to eat and their foul smell and the fact that they were all crowding round me, made me want to throw up, but I couldn't. It was already afternoon when they brought me a little milk and some bread, but I refused to take them. I tried to make them believe that I was pregnant, but I could not manage it. I noticed that they began to feel sorry for me and from then on they stopped tormenting me.

Then I tried to find an opportunity to appear once more before the King, who was sleeping. Again I made my way with those women through the long dark corridors until we reached the place where the royal chamber was and I still pretended to be as ill as ever. One of the royal capons was there – they are blacks kept to guard the King's women in his house. This capon knew a little Spanish and asked me what was wrong. I told him that I was pregnant and wanted to go back to my brothers[39] since I was not well. He then spoke to the women who were with me before answering and then he said that the King had entrusted me to them to make me turn Turk before I was brought back to his presence. I pretended to be very unwell, for I noticed the women began to have pity on me and even more when they learned that I was pregnant, which in fact I was not. They did not torment me any more and sat by me, pointing to the sky as if to say that God would provide.

I had not been there long before the King came out of his chamber and the women took me, one by one arm, one by the other, and the third took the little dog and the fourth took the zither and thus they led me before the King. I was now very glad to have done with it, dead or free, but God commands all and saved me from his hands. I prostrated myself before the King without fear. I expected nothing from him but a mortal blow. He pushed me away and I got up and ran after him and prostrated myself for the second time and begged him to leave me with my brothers. He pushed me away again and then I got up for the third time and ran after him as far as the portal through which the King was to go out, and I threw myself at his feet again and said:

"Cut my throat, I prefer that to turning Turk."

The King, seeing my self-assurance and my courage like that of a lion and that I was preventing him from going out of his palace, gave me a most terrible look and stopped and at last spoke to the women who were supposed to escort him and especially the four who had brought me before him, who all told him that I was pregnant, that I had eaten nothing all day and from time to time I was like one dead, but then came back to life and they begged the King to let me go. I could not understand that, but after I had learned the language and come to frequent the royal palace, they told it to the sister of the King in my presence. I could see, though, that they were on my side. The King, after listening to what the women had to say, turned to me and said that four men would come for me to take me to my brothers. He said this in Spanish, so that I could understand it clearly and then I got up at once and let the King pass.

The women then began to show great pleasure, giving cries of joy and made signs that I should come back and visit them. I pretended to agree to everything and thought: if I manage to get out of here, I shan't be back so soon. I was happy to have managed to escape so far, but the Christians were mortally troubled and uneasy, for they feared that I had turned Turk. Especially the Christian with whom I was lodging, for he was afraid that his wife would have to go to the palace every day to teach me the language, because she was born in the country and knew the language as well as the Turks. So there was no little grief among the Christians and the Fathers when they saw the King appear and not me. This lasted for a good half hour after the departure of the King, before a capon came to fetch me and lead me to the Christians.

As soon as I left the King's house, I saw a real army of the King's bodyguards all armed and not a single Christian. Then I thought:

"What awaits me? Now I am going to be killed!"

For one could have no faith in the King, as he was a great tyrant and for him killing a dozen people before breakfast was of no importance. So I was approaching the bodyguards, when Jan Catallana arrived and snatched me from the capon, with malicious and insulting words. As soon as I saw him, I was as pleased as if I had been set free. He took me by the hand and led me through the whole of the royal guard, until we reached the room where the Christians lived who were in charge of watching over the King's warehouses. He shut me in there. It was about sunset that they had to fetch the arms. At this point the head of the Dutch arrived to ask me what had happened to me when I was with the King. I told him briefly that I had been turned over to be made a Turk and that God had saved me from it and that it was impossible for me to tell him everything, but that later I would relate it all in detail. He told me that everyone who was in the warehouse, Christians and Turks alike, imagined that I had turned Turk and that Jan Catallana had been very afraid of it. For then his wife would have been exposed to the danger of having to go to the palace every day to instruct me in the language and they had been very distressed by this, not without reason. We could not exchange many words, because the leader had to help gather up the arms.

**Remarriage**

I then remained alone in this chamber with my thoughts and I addressed myself to God, whom I thanked for His grace which had supported me and because I had greatly preferred a cruel death to turning Turk. I had scarcely finished my prayer when I was called again to the King and I went very much at my ease and not in the least afraid. So I found myself before him once again and I went to sit down outside the door to his chamber to play [the zither], while the King and his brothers and the Bashi refreshed themselves inside by eating watermelons. He was at that time happy and cheerful among his companions, which gave me the courage to reach out to attain my aim. After I had played for some time, the King had me stop and said to the Christian who had led me before the King that he should ask me what I wanted, and he asked. I replied that he should tell the King that I wanted Pieter, the head of the Dutch nation. I then spoke the name of the leader so that he could not cheat me in front of the King, given that it was not what he desired. He then answered the King in my name saying that I begged God and my master to be allowed to marry my compatriot. The King said:

"Go and fetch him."

Meanwhile the King had clearly made out the name Pieter in what I said and as soon as the chamberlain appeared before him, he asked him if he was really called Pieter. He answered yes and he asked him whether he was my fellow countryman. He said yes; and if he wanted to take me as his wife. He said:

"If it so please God and Your Majesty."

At which, the King said:

"I give her to you, take good care of her", three times over.

I did not hear anything of this conversation, for the chamberlain was standing behind me and he thanked the King and was preparing to leave when he called me, but I did not hear. The King, noticing this, called:

"Come here, Pieter."

This he did immediately and the King said to him three times: "Take her by the hand."

He then took me by the hand, which I drew away immediately. He then took me by the hand a second time and told me the King had given me to him, so I turned around and saw who it was who said that to me and saw it was the right man. So I well nigh forgot the King and went away without thanking him because I was so happy.

So we went together into the room where there were also the Bashis and other important people. We stayed there until the King had returned to his quarters.

It was already past sunset when we left there and went directly to the monastery of the Fathers, where we were married then and there. But before we could be married, my husband first had to be baptized after the Roman manner, because they don't believe that the Reformed or Lutheran are baptized. Yes, they dare to say that the Turks are better than the aforementioned, because the Turks say they believe in God and the Reformed and the Lutherans do not, telling many monstrous and blasphemous lies about them.

## Trouble Makers

So, we were married according to the customs of this country and we set out at once for the house of Jan Catallana, where we had a splendid marriage feast with six eggs and a small round loaf of the size you get here for a *stuyver*[40]. And after that, my new husband went to his house and I stayed where I was and that evening I had to put up with more insults and offence from the people of the house, more than I could endure, and this was because I had not done what they wanted, and it got worse from day to day. They tried to make trouble between my husband and me, but it never worked, because the fox was too cunning for them. On all sides there was nothing but thorns and prickles and I cannot describe how much they stung us. I will only give a few examples. They tried to stir me up against my husband, saying that he only married through sheer laziness, so as not to have to work and so as to have more opportunities to chase whores and that he had money, but made me believe he hadn't. They brought witnesses who would confirm it on oath, but I still remained very sceptical of all they said, for I did not believe without having seen and felt it, in spite of all the tricks and all the stratagems they set for me. It was all in vain and Jan Catallana got angry and said:

"You are capable, with your intelligence of betraying the whole world."

That was because after sowing all these tares, he did not harvest the fruit he would have liked: in other words, I did not become disgusted with my husband and give him a kick to get rid of him. And they said to my husband that I did things that were not decent and proper for a respectable woman.

Dear reader, you can imagine what our state of mind was like at times. We were strangers to each other, we had never known each other before, we had never heard anything about each other, nor yet about our families. We were like alien birds – one does not know where they came from, nor what their origins were; it was as if we had fallen from the sky. I wished over and over again not to have to stay on in this house, but to live alone with my husband. But he couldn't find a way.

## Keeping a Tavern

At the end of three months, I went to visit the Jew mentioned above, who lived at the Bashi's house. There I complained of everything I had to suffer in the house of that Spaniard and asked if there were not a possibility that I could find a house to rent and live there, but the opportunity did not arise. My husband kept a tavern in a stable, in the middle of the animals and it had such a desolate air that the worst stables looked like palaces in comparison, so that my husband did not want me to go there. But I asked my husband so insistently to visit the tavern that in the end he decided to go with me. So we got to the tavern, which was really wretched, and I decided then and there to stay. My husband was opposed, but it made no difference. I preferred to live in peace in that disgusting hole and eat dry bread, or whatever God saw fit to send us, rather than in the Spanish house, where I did not have to worry about eating, but was always in the midst of arguments. I remained immovable and my husband had to go at once and fetch all my things from the Spanish house. My husband and I didn't have much and we had to make do with living very modestly. However, God helped us and even before Christmas in that same year, 1732, His Excellency Frans van der Meer, Ambassador at the Court of Spain, sent me 50 *rijxsdaalers*[41]. This was most welcome, for I was pregnant with my first child and needed everything, and everything was dear and we didn't even earn enough to live.

## Some Help from the Queen

We stayed on in this stable until the end of April, 1732, when the King's mother returned from her pilgrimage to Megcha [Mecca], where, according to what she said, Magomet [Muhammad] is buried.[42] A French merchant had arrived at Salé with a gift to buy back French slaves. I was chosen to take the gift to the Queen with the request for liberation, as well as flattering comments to that effect. They had one who was a mistress of languages accompany me and I made use of her. I had a written petition in which I congratulated the Queen and also begged her to find me a house. As soon as I had finished my task for the Ambassador, I gave my letter to the Queen who at once gave me this house and she appointed several people to go with me, who went to the headmen of the town with orders to give me the house. But this resulted in the great enmity of the Fathers, who had promised me the house of this Spanish woman. But the bird was too clever for her, for I knew in advance that no Frenchman would be freed, let alone any Spaniard. But the King, not daring to send the Ambassador away with no one, freed six old Frenchmen because of the gift, but [he] still had to pay 600 *rijksdaalders* for each one.

I settled into the house that I had received from the Queen, but it was in such a state that I couldn't live there without making some repairs. I spent 14 ducats on this house to be able to live in it and scarcely was it in a fit state than I had to leave it again. In this way, we had spent, at the beginning of the year, the month of February, which was the month of Ramadan[43] or fasting for the Moors or Turks, in the house of the Bashi, with this Jew because during the fast the Moors and Turks do not drink strong drinks. When we set out for our stable, this Jew reproached me, among other things, with my having gone to the Bashi to stir him up and make him take away his - the Jew's - house, which was something just as impossible as for someone to touch the sky with their hand, because everything depended on the King and not on a Bashi, who was in no position to drive out Christians and put someone else in their place; and I had never seen this Bashi. This Jew held to what he claimed and although we swore that we were innocent in this matter, it was in vain. So then we tried not to be dependant any longer on a Bashi, but we tried to depend on the Queen, so as not to run the danger of having to give royal service.

Nevertheless, on the 29th June of this same year 1732, the King had brought before him all the Christian slaves. They also came to our house, to fetch my husband and me to appear before the King. As soon as we had arrived at the King's palace, we left the others and went to the Queen to beg her to take my husband on as a gatekeeper. The Queen granted me this and she sent my husband and me with two messengers to the town, to the chief of the slaves. I had a lot of trouble going there, because I was at the end of my pregnancy and so I risked giving birth along the way. I went home with much effort while my husband went to the monastery to fetch something and there he found a messenger of the King with orders to take my husband and me to the Bashi mentioned above, for the King had taken the Jew away from the Bashi and had replaced him with my husband and me, completely against our will. For the King, after having inspected all the Christians and distributed them according to his whim, had asked the leader of the Christians if all the Christians were there and this leader answered that all the Christians were there except for the husband and wife whom the King had married. At which the King said:

"I took two Christians away from the Bashi, give the Bashi this man and woman in their place."

We, and the messengers of the Queen, tried to persuade the messenger to let us escape this order, but the royal word overruled all others and it was with the greatest displeasure that we were forced to give in. And so this was why we had to leave our little house over which we had been to so much expense and which I then gave to another woman, a Portuguese, to live in as long as we didn't need it. The Bashi was good to the Christians and was kind to them and said to the Jew that if he wanted to stay, he could remain in the house, that we would give him a room where he could sleep; and this is what we did.

There was a tavern attached to this house that the Bashi had agreed to give to his Christians to enable them to earn their living, which therefore reverted to us and we were not obliged to share it with anyone at all, though we had to go to the expense of a manservant and brooms for the Bashi's house, for my husband had the task of sweeping the Bashi's house and street, and the tavern had to provide for all the expenses connected with this. We made an agreement with the Jew: if he wanted to stay, that he should have one third of the profits of the tavern and furthermore his food and drink every day, so that he was fed for free and paid on top of that, with the money for which my husband and I had to work, while he did not have to do it, since he was working in the King's service from the rising until the setting of the sun.

He agreed, but it did not last for long because we could not tolerate his bringing Turkish women into the house at night, because our lives would have been forfeit, if it were discovered. For that reason he left us, which didn't grieve us in the least, since we were no longer in danger. And so we lived a year and a half with the Bashi, and our tavern did nicely, so that we were not too unhappy. We also suffered a number of indignities, which I shall not dwell on but leave out of my life story, and proceed to the essentials, to which end I began this little book on the 28th of October, 1733.

**A Change of Masters**

Very early in the morning, as was the custom, all the Bashis and leaders waited on the King before the door of the palace, and our Bashi formed part of his guard. When the King came out, he had the Bashi sit down before him and had his head shattered by his men, so that he died, and he seized the Bashi's house and furnishings and even his slaves and Christians. The women were chased out into the street with nothing, so that we were once again in the hands of the King. For, on the last day of that year, my husband was put to work in the service of the King and it was such work that many Christians and Moors died while doing it, so that my husband too was in great danger of losing his life. I too was forced to leave the house; it is true I had another where I could live, but I could not throw the Portuguese woman out of it; but I went to lodge temporarily with another Christian, while waiting to get another [house] from the Queen. Every day I did my best to free my husband from this work in the service of the King. They promised me a lot, but in truth I did not get my husband. I then got another house, but I had to pay the rent and couldn't make any money, but nonetheless there had to be food on the table, for we had nothing except what a good friend lent us, until God provided.

**Maria ter Meetelen Protests**

I thought: "It can't go on like this; we must try something" and I risked a good beating and I stole out of the house secretly on the 9th of March in the year 1734. It was a Friday, the day when the King went to Church [sic] for that is their Sunday [sic]. As I was going out of the door of our *bagnio*, the guard asked me where I was going; I answered:
"To the market for meat".
He believed me and let me go. I had my second little child, eight months old, in my arms and when I got to the market a butcher's boy

snatched off his little bonnet. I seized the boy and wanted to drag him before the King, when all the people gathered and begged and implored me to let him go. Observing this, I decided to go into the matter more deeply and insisted loudly on taking him, thinking:

"This is a good beginning; I am going to be brave, full of assurance and courageous" – and I was.

So I went to the palace of the King, but I could not go in because the King had already left his house to go to the Church so that I had to go round the outside walls and the citadel to enter the palace by another door. But there I was exposed to the danger of running into the overseers of the works, under whom the Christians, of whom my husband was one, were labouring, and I found him there. I was not without great fear, but I took the risk of being given a sound beating, and my husband too, as well as being put in irons. So I managed the affair very cleverly. When I approached those overseers and those Christians, they asked me where I was going. I said that the Queen had summoned me for this day. And that she would ask the King for my husband, and I said that quite innocently. They didn't manage to learn anything else from me and they said I was doing the right thing and they gave their permission. For they knew that the Queen had very little influence with the King and that I would not succeed in freeing my husband through her, something of which I myself was well aware, but I did not let it show. For I had already been going to see the Queen for four months, at great expense, with no result, so that I was looking for another subterfuge to gain my ends.

So, I went in through the palace door and on inside until I was just by the other door through which the King had passed to go to the Church. I waited there in the great courtyard of the palace until the King came out of the Church, but he could not cross this square but went out of the door and took the same exterior route that I had taken earlier. I was thus forced to go through the interior again to go to the other door, which I did. I got through with great difficulty and arrived on the path where the King was to pass. However, the overseers of the Christians had noticed me and asked my husband if I wanted to come before the King. But he pretended to know nothing about it. They sent my husband to me to tell me that I should go into one of these old houses. But before he had gone ten paces, the King appeared at the corner of the citadel, which forced my husband to go back to his work immediately. As for myself, I approached the King and placed myself in the middle of the road so that the King would see me from a distance and so that none of the guards who went before the

*The Grain Market at Meknès – postcard c.1910*

King could chase me away. The King approached me and already, while he was still at a distance, I prostrated myself and cried:

"*Lyber vameryk asiede*"[44], which means: "May Allah protect the head of my Lord."

And I kissed the earth, so that my face retained traces of it, as is the custom when one appears before the King. The King, seeing this, treated me graciously and sent two men to ask me what I wanted. I told them that I wanted to talk to the King himself and I did not want to tell them. Then they took me before the King. I didn't have the patience to wait until he questioned me, but I cried at the top of my voice:

"May Allah protect the head of my Lord. My Lord has given me a good husband."

The King took a lively interest in me and said to his Bashis:

"Isn't this the Christian I gave to that Bashi? Go and get him and give them to the Christian who guards my warehouses and order him to allot them a house and give them food and let the husband work to feed his wife and child."

One of the Bashis immediately came forward and seized me by the hand and led me away from the King and had one of his menservants fetch my husband and take us to this Christian, who was ordered to help us as the King had said.

**Jealousy**

But we were still far from being home and dry. While my husband should have worked to feed me and the child, my husband was forced to work for him [the Christian] and, on top of that, give him money. The Moors, having seen my courage and daring, decided to show me a little courtesy and no longer dared to treat me so harshly, although up to then they had greatly oppressed me in every way. And from that time on, I became a little bolder towards them and ceaselessly asked the King for things. And from that time, they no longer harassed me, which made the Spanish woman very jealous; she set to work with all sorts of tricks and lies, by means of the Queen's messenger-woman, trying in all ways to get her foot on my neck so that every time I went to the Queen there were lots of complaints about me. First of all, I had had in my keeping a coffer belonging to my Bashi with silver and other goods and, entrusted with keeping it, I had not made it over to the King. Again, my child had just died. So, she said I had killed my child. When she saw that I was not punished as she wished, she found or invented something else, but I was not bothered, for a horse that is not mangy does not fear the spur. I did not stop going to visit the Queen.

## Another Christian Woman Makes Trouble

In the meantime, through the Queen's messenger woman, she had arranged it that she should be the head of all the Christian women living in the land. There were five of us: I and two Portuguese and she and her old mother, and all should be under her like winter corn lying in the field. But I was too free for her, so she used every trick to try to get me under her power, making out that she was afraid that I would run away, just like a man and woman and their family had run away, but it gave her no hold over me; I was not controllable enough for her.

I was then, one morning, commanded by her in the name of the Queen that I and she must make an appearance. I hesitated to go, because in my sleep I had had a dream in which I foresaw everything that would happen to me on that day. I then got three different commands, but I didn't want to go, so my man pressed me to go. I didn't go without wet eyes, because of my premonitions that I would meet with something wicked. I tried to go first to the Queen, but she had set out guards, so that I could not and I soon found myself in her [the Christian woman] company.

She smeared her mouth with honeyed words, but the dog was too old and didn't bite the stick: I let it go in one ear and out the other. The Christians there that the King had given to replace us also oppressed us, but God supported us, so that all her tricks and lies came to nothing.

We then came to the Queen's palace. I was used to going straight to the Queen's chamber whenever I came to the Palace, but with her this wasn't so, so we had to sit there a long time, until the evening, which distressed me.

She was soon with me, when the Queen said to me: " I have made this high born woman the head-person", whereupon I was very bold in my answer and said that I recognized no-one except God and the King and herself, and that one slave couldn't rule over another, and that I appealed to God and herself that I should be under her and not under a slave, because she was no more than me and I was no more than her. Whereupon the Queen asking me under whose rule I was in my land, I said: "Under God and my parents" and that I was also willing to be ruled by her and the King. Whereupon the Queen said to her to leave me in peace and that I was accountable to her [the Queen].

But that wasn't enough for her, and she brought up other accusations and said that she was afraid that I would run away, just like it had once happened there with a woman who had run away with her family and come safely to Christian lands[45] and that she and her family would therefore suffer. The Queen was much impressed by this, but I said:

"Her Majesty has never heard that a Hollander or an Englishman has run away, it is the Spaniards and the Portuguese, because they have a foothold in the land where they can be made free, but we would only be in worse slavery there than we are now here with her Majesty."

That satisfied the Queen as to the question of my freedom but for the third time she [the woman] pressed another point, because she saw that she couldn't win with the preceding one.

She herself didn't speak with the Queen, but the Queen's messenger, who she had bribed, spoke her words for her. She had been born in the land and was of the King's blood, through two sisters of her mother who had married the old King, so that she was called aunt[46] by the royal children, and she spoke the language as well as any from that land, and I didn't know the language at all, so many times I was thinking how I would be able to make an answer.

Nevertheless, I took heart from my faith, that God guides a man's tongue to say what he must. She then said to the Queen that the King had given me and my husband to her husband. I said in a forceful manner:

"She is lying, for the King gave me and my husband to the Christians at the King's warehouse, where her husband was also only a worker, just like my husband was".

The Queen, seeing that she was trying to set her foot on my neck, charged her that she should leave me in peace and not to hit her head against mine and so sent us away, and ordered her treasurer to give us a pair of ducats. We came outside of the Queen's chamber, where we stood waiting until the Queen's treasurer came with the two ducats, which took a long time, so I started to leave. She wanted me to stay but I didn't trust her and let my part of the money go, and I went immediately to our head to whom the King had given me and my husband, and told him how she had tried to put me under her command and how I had protected myself. About half an hour later she came there herself; she put herself beside me. She was angry beyond reason and didn't know any more how she could catch me out, in order to make me angry too - but the fox was too sly for her. When she saw that she couldn't get a hold on me, she said that she had been given 10 ducats, and if I had been there too I would have got as much. I couldn't bear these terrible lies, whereupon I said that she was lying and had only got two ducats, whereupon she stood up and I sat down on the ground, as is the custom there because they have no chairs or benches.

She then treacherously came up to me as I sat by the post of the door as if she wanted to go inside, and she kicked me in the neck so hard that I couldn't stand up. I had never before experienced anything like it. I wasn't brought up to fight. I ran out and went to another room, where the Christians kept their cooked food, where I found one of my fellow ship's passengers, whom I beseeched to take me to my home, and waited there until she had gone away. And then I went to my headman, who was a Frenchman and as treacherous as could be; I asked him whether it was fair and if he wouldn't look after my rights. He thought about this, because he himself wanted to set his foot on our neck, but he didn't have the power, because fat floats above water, and it's the same with justice.

## The End of the First Reign of Moulay Abdallah (1731-34) The Reign of Moulay Ali al Aredj (1735-6)

We did not keep the King Muly Abdela [Moulay Abdallah] for very long. For a month after this business, the King returned from the army and the English Ambassador[47] came for his slaves on the 11th of August in the year 1734. And on the 12th, which was the King's Easter[48] for slaughtering the lamb, which took place outside the town on a hill, where the King in person cut the throat of the paschal lamb. And it is supposed to be still alive when it reaches the palace and if it was dead they prophesied that the King would not be king for much longer and they put the lamb on a mule which trotted along briskly to bring it to the palace. The mule stumbled on the way and all the important men saw it, at which they bowed their heads and prophesied that the King would soon reach the end of his reign, which was indeed the case. The King, on his way back from the paschal celebration, had to pass behind the cloister of the Fathers, which was against the walls of the town and the English ambassador stood at the top of his house with musicians and greeted the King who returned his greeting with three salvos of musketry.

On the following day, the Ambassador presented himself before the King with his gifts and asked for his slaves and he obtained them all and even others over and above: Scots, Irish and Hanoverians[49], who were living in Holland and had been captured while fighting under Dutch colours, so that he obtained 146 slaves with whom he left the town that very day, and about the same time there was a merchant there as well called Joseph Rebexo[50], who was engaged in negotiations with the King for eight Dutch slaves, in other words: captains, a pilot and a passenger, one of whom was my captain.

The agreement was reached on the 16th of September and as there was still a captain who had to come 100 miles from Tafilelt[51], the others could not leave, because in the meantime the King had been deposed and saved himself by fleeing. And immediately it was Muly Elle [Moulay Ali al Aredj] who was proclaimed King and he was a terrible tyrant for Christians and Moors. He brought this captain back with him, but he did not break the agreement, but granted liberty to these eight slaves as had been established.

**Insults and Worse**

It so happened that I had had to put up with trouble from the brother of the King and from the *bailli* or Governor of this town. They obliged me to pay taxes on the house and every day they demanded more, making difficulties for me, and it was a house that I had received from the previous King and they did not dare get their hands on it, but my husband had to pay for it with blows. And so it happened that one morning the Governor called my husband to the door and demanded money from him. And then my husband answered that he had already paid several months in advance; the Governor insulted him and called him *keffer*[52] and horned beast and a took a stick and hit him hard. As I was standing there in the entrance, I ran forward and freed my husband. This Governor continued his ride, as soon as I intervened, without speaking of the matter. I threatened him with the King and that I would complain to him, but my husband kept on holding me back, because he was a great tyrant and could well have me shot without even listening to me. But I paid no attention to him. As my husband was in the King's warehouse during the day, I would have plenty of opportunity to go to the King without my husband knowing anything about it. So, on the following day, I carried out my plan without anyone's knowledge. In the morning, I went to the King before he had left his palace and I waited at the gate of the town. And while I was standing there, a slave from Dunkerque came with two Moors to give these Moors, in the presence of the King, the chain for the King's lions and bears, so as not to have to pay for it twice[53]. He was about twenty paces away from me when the King approached. At about ten paces, the King said:

"What does that infidel want? Go and sniff him to see if he has drunk alcohol."

The Moors did not dare say anything other than:

"He has drunk alcohol; he stinks of *eau de vie*."

The King, without even asking why the Christian had come to him, shot at him and killed him. When I saw that, I fled towards the town before it should be my turn. I barely escaped for I could not get to the town fast enough and the King was already at the outer gate. When my husband learned of this, he was in equal measure astonished and frightened by such great self-assurance. This King was also a great tyrant in his heart, for he had a good number of Christians executed and buried under the olive trees[54]. Then he spread the rumour that they had run away, so that it would be well seen by the old King, his father – this was while he was still a prince - and thus he obtained other Christians [from him]. He was King for 19 months and during that time he had five innocent Christians killed and he shot a hundred and twenty balls into one of them, as I will tell in due course, as well as the fact that he tried to kill my husband.

About a month later, the married men and women were called before him. We were four couples and a mother with her son; we were exempt from work, except for the husband of the woman of whom I have already spoken whose hate towards me increased yet more, but she was afraid of me because I did not hesitate to go to the King so that she left me in peace. We were about to enter a sad period of high prices, for an *alemout*, that is to say a measure of 10 or 11 pounds of wheat, cost thirty *dubbeltjes*[55] and previously we had only paid one and a half *dubbeltjes* for a measure. But people had money and there was some trade so we did not suffer as in the most recent period of high prices, which will be described later.

## Summoned by the King

In the mean time, the King left us in peace until the 4th of February of the year 1735 when the King summoned the married people. Now, there was there one of the Portuguese women whose husband had died that very morning and I had given birth about a month before and had swaddled my child in the Dutch manner. Now the King said to the woman: "Go and fetch me the cushion which that Christian has in her arms!" She took the child from me and carried it to the King who was much astonished, for he thought it was a cushion and I was very uneasy indeed. After having examined it for quite a long time, he called my husband, gave him the child and asked his nationality. He said that he was Dutch. And the King told him that if he had money to buy his freedom, he should tell the King, which was a word of consolation for the other women, who had all been told the opposite, apart from the young widow, who received the order to go home until the King gave her another husband. I was given, together with a Portuguese woman, to the sister of the King called Silla bint Mulay[56] and the Spanish woman and her mother to the youngest sister of the King.

I was very happy with my mistress, much more so than my companion, but the worst of all was that I went in fear to the palace, because the youngest brother of the King always held a knife to my breast and said:

"Turn Turk or it goes in".

And several times he spat in my face and beat me and hit me so that I hardly dared go to the palace. I did not dare complain to the King, for we were in a period when we were esteemed less than the Jews and they care more for a dog than a Jew, so that we had to put up with all sorts of wrongs done to us and reward them with gifts and presents. And when one of the Moors among the King's people had got drunk it was us, the slaves, who had to pay for it and shut our taverns and pay out money on top of everything else. The Moors seeing this had every occasion to despoil the Christians and milk them at will.

## Jean Pusole

There was there, among others, a tavern-keeper of the French nation and some Moors came to his place with a young boy and they wanted to have a room just for them. This tavern-keeper – his name was Jean Pusole – did not want to agree, so they menaced him with reprisals and in fact carried out their threats. By night they came to our *bagnio* or *knoo* and dragged Jean Pusole from his bed, took him before the King and in the morning, at the first hour, they accused him of allowing people into his house to commit sins.

The King, being opposed to this, took his gun and fired five shots at him without hitting him and at the sixth shot it jammed, which made the King very angry and he threw his gun on the ground and ordered his men to fire on him [Jean Pusole]. He was surrounded by a hundred and twenty men who all had their guns charged with balls and they all fired at him, but not a single ball did him any harm, except his clothes where they went through. When the King saw that not one single one of the balls had hit him, he sent him back to the *knoo* to be stripped of everything. He had nothing, because he was a servant of the French nation, but they did not want to understand and began to beat him terribly with cords of leather, soaked and knotted and so he was forced to give them all the money that belonged to the French community. And the leader of the community who kept the money was also appallingly ill-treated.

The Fathers, on finding about this affair, tried to interpose but in vain and they were even obliged to prepare a gift for the King and they went there [to him]. Besides, there was an old slave who was first class at making guns for the King and who had great influence with all the kings because of his skill at this work. He always had gun barrels ready as presents for the King when some slave fell into disgrace with the King, for which reason many slaves owed him their lives.

So this old slave, accompanied by the Fathers, went with the Moors who had the Christians' money before the King and gave him the present and asked for permission to speak to the King, which was granted them and they explained about the matter saying that Jean Pisole [sic] was in the service of the French nation and that he was a poor man, owning nothing, and that the money they had found in his keeping belonged to the community and, thanks to it, they made wine every year, and it was used for clothing and food, and from time to time money was distributed to members of the community, and with it the sick and wounded were cared for, and that truly there were yet other things that the money was used for. They obtained from the King the return of the money and the freeing of Jean Pisole – but it cost at least half the money. This took place in the October of the year 1735, while my husband was at Salé with the Dutch Ambassador, Heer Henderik Lynslager[57].

## Ransoming Slaves – Diplomatic Difficulties

Now, on June 27th we had received a letter according to which the gentleman mentioned above was coming with a present for the King with a view to ransoming us, us slaves. And as Heer Lynslager had left Holland when Muly Abdela was still King and had received orders that he should disembark so as to negotiate verbally with the King concerning

*The Armourers Soukh in Meknès – postcard c.1920.*

peace and the freeing of slaves and this gentleman did not realize that there was a new King, something which he only noted on his arrival and the gentleman mentioned above could not make up his mind to disembark before their High Lordships[58] were informed of the matter and had given their orders.

As soon as the King was informed that the Dutch Ambassador was in the Bay of Salé, the King invited him to disembark and negotiate with him verbally and he would grant him the slaves on condition that he came personally to receive them. But the Ambassador sent his excuses saying that he had no orders to land, at which point the King sent my husband to persuade the Ambassador. But it was in vain and not long after my husband, the King sent a Bashi with 40 men to escort him on the road, so that he need not be afraid. But it was in vain, for Heer Lynslager first wanted to obtain the slaves and then send the gift and silver to land, as had been agreed, but this would never have been possible and indeed it was not. Heer Lynslager sent us a list of the presents for the King and indeed they were very fine and valuable and we had it translated into the Turkish language[59] and thus it was presented to the King, who was very pleased. And it was valued at twenty *cintaals* [60] of silver and each *cintaal* was worth a thousand silver ducats and each ducat was three and a half florins by Dutch reckoning; but it was no good: the King did not give in.

**Portuguese Fathers and their Gifts**

Meanwhile, the Ambassador went to Cadix [Cadiz] to write to their High Lordships about this matter and to await orders to disembark. The King called his Bashi. Among others, Portuguese Fathers arrived with a special ambassador from Tangiers with a present of three lacquered cabinets and an assortment of porcelain from Delft which we, in our country, display in cabinets, and a certain quantity of tea and sugar and preserves, all of which was not worth a tenth of the High Lordships' present. All this now seemed no more than a wretched gift.

He arrived on the 17th September at Meknès; on the 18th he appeared before the King. And he was received very civilly by the King. He was set on a horse with a golden saddle and thus he rode with the King across the whole palace to visit it and he was immediately given his slaves, who were already handed over to him on the morning of the 19th, 73 in all. And on the 20th, he bade farewell to the King and set out for Salé where he embarked on the 24th. We were not a little sad to see these Portuguese go - and for such a small price⁶¹, while we had to stay; and greater grief was to follow. For my husband was still in Salé and could not come back until the King summoned him; and he had him fetched in a great rage.

At the end of November the King, being somewhat unwell, asked the Christian doctor to come and give him a purge. He prescribed his spending the day quietly and keeping warm, for otherwise the purge would not work and would do him harm. And this is what happened, for the King did just the opposite and in the afternoon he was very ill. Then he called the Master back and also some Turkish Masters⁶² and asked the Master what stuff he had administered to him. The Master told the King and the Masters the medicine and that the King himself was the reason he was ill and that it was his own fault at which the King became furious and said:

"You have designs on my life?"

He had the Master step back three or four paces, took his gun and killed him and ordered all his people to shoot at the head of the Master until it was unrecognizable. He had him carried in this state to the Christians' forge.

## Maria's Husband Blamed

In the meantime, he had remembered my husband and asked:

"Where is that infidel who was supposed to fetch the Ambassador, his Christian brother?"

When he learned it, he sent a bodyguard to fetch him to have him suffer the same fate as the doctor. For the King accused my husband of having advised the Ambassador not to disembark. So, while the bodyguard was absent fetching my husband, and it was at least six days before he came back, the King became more and more ill, so that he could only talk with his brothers and his Bashis, which was good luck for us. If that had not happened, my husband would have been led before the King as soon as he reached the town, without even being able to speak to his wife. So he arrived at the town on December 5ᵗʰ towards evening, prepared to die. He had ardently beseeched God to be able to talk to me and to make over to me some money, which he had received from Heer Lynslager and from the Captains and the Commander, for otherwise it would have been loot for the Turks. He had the luck to be sent home because night was falling and he could not appear before the King. But he had to go before the King on the following day.

Meanwhile, the Fathers had had time to order a present for the King from the head of the King's forge and also to square the matter with the Bashis to some extent and to find excuses for my husband: that he, being a slave, could not force the Ambassador to disembark; that he bitterly regretted not seeing him on land; that several letters had been sent to Holland to receive the order to disembark and then to negotiate verbally with the King, but it took a great deal of time, at least 3 or 4 months. The affair was approved by the Bashis, but it remained to be seen how the King would take it. We spent that night in the greatest sadness and in the morning it was as if we had said farewell forever and as if they were snatching away my husband to lead him like a lamb to the slaughterhouse. The honoured reader can imagine in what distress I found myself, for I was in the last three months of pregnancy with my son.

The Fathers and the heads of the forge walked in front, each bearing a gift and they suborned the brother of the King by promising to reward him if my husband kept his life. But he was not satisfied until it had been decided what he would receive. They came to an agreement for 20 ducats and a pair of silk stockings as well as a gift from the Fathers and the heads[63]. When they had reached an agreement, he accepted the Fathers' present, which consisted of tea, porcelain, sugar and preserves. The present of the Master [craftsman] was a magnificent gun barrel with which he himself presented himself before the King. This gift slightly softened the King's heart, for he was very greedy and the proverb: "The sea has never said 'I have had enough', nor the womb 'too much'" could be applied to him. The King changed his mind; he pardoned my husband and it seemed that we were born anew. The joy was now not less great than the grief, for I saw my husband raised from the dead before me. This lasted a short time, as we will see.

## The Country in Revolt

The King's health recovered and the country was in revolt, for these wanted this king, and those the other. We Christians also passionately wanted another King, as no one among us was sure of his life. For, during the last month of his reign, he asked one of our slaves who was guarding the warehouse, if there was not someone among his brothers chained up, so that he could wash his gun in his blood. It was not enough for him to attempt our lives, but he did not even want to let us earn our bread. For our taverns were closed and we could only sell secretly, trembling with fear; and we paid a lot of fines, so that we would soon have become very poor. However, God provided, for there was again a change among the Blacks[64] some of whom wanted to make one king and some another. The country people refused to pay their tribute, so that the King was obliged to set out on campaign, which he did on 24th April of the year 1736. But he came back quickly on the 27th April, said goodbye to his wife and children and fled with his brother and son. When we learned this, not knowing which King would be proclaimed, we were afraid of rioting that would end in theft and pillage. So, we took refuge in the palace and buried anything we possessed and there we stayed until the first of May. Early in the morning, Mulay Abdela was proclaimed king with much cheering. His son, who was at the palace, was immediately set on a horse – on a horse with a golden saddle and with a parasol[65] over his head and was named regent, to our great regret, for he made the Christians labour very hard.

## The second reign of Moulay Abdallah (1736)
## Moulay Muhammad (1736-8)

### Four Kings in a Day

I went immediately to the mother of the King who had been imprisoned all this time. I had sometimes visited her in prison, which had pleased her. I congratulated her and then went into town to my house and thought that peace had come. But this was absolutely not the case, for before it was midday we had already had four kings. One after another was put on the throne and then deposed, with a result that there were considerable skirmishes at the palace. We were again several days without a King until the 8th of May when Mulay Abdela was once more proclaimed King and brought back from Tétula[66] where he was with a considerable army, six days journey from the town. In mid-June he approached the town and reached his palace, but he did not stay long for he left at once and went outside the city where he had a small palace[67], or summer residence, about three hours from the town and there he summoned all the Christian slaves who had to labour and dig a trench[68] all round the palace. All the Christians went there and there was no one left but the Spanish woman and her mother, myself and my child, and the priests in their cloister.

I stayed there with my child without a *stuyver* in the world with which to feed my child and myself. And to stay alone in the house with the

Moors made me equally afraid. The Christian who sometimes would lend ten ducats had also left in haste, and he did not even have the time to extract a little money from the *matamoras*[69]. That is a hole in the ground where we hid various things because of the Turks, according to the custom of the country, where the inhabitants hide everything under ground because of the enemy. In this great distress, I fled to the cloister with all I had and at once they gave me a room and as much food and drink as I wanted.

I was very well off there, but I was very unhappy knowing how much my husband had to suffer and also the other Christians. For they were made to work very hard in the full sun, excavating and blowing up mines and what they had to eat was barely a little one *stuyver* roll of bread and sometimes nothing at all, and at night they slept under the stars and drank stinking water, so that before the end of the month all the Christians were ill with the result that there were only eight or nine working. And the King did not want the Christians to be taken to the town to heal them, until he saw that they were dying like mosquitoes. It was only then that he allowed it. On the 17th of June, 220 Christians set out, and on the 20th September only 100 were left, both sick and well. On the 24th August, we had already lost 24 of the Dutch nation. My husband, among others, had already come back to the house twice ill, and it cost me a lot of money to be able to care for him at home.

## Another Tavern

I had been about six days at the monastery when the Bashis returned to the town coming from the expedition. I took my child in my arms and went at once to the palace without saying anything to anyone, because I knew they would stop me going there, and I presented myself before the Bashi and asked permission to open my tavern again in order to be able to earn my bread and that of my husband and child, and also to be able to collect my rations from the King, which the Bashi granted me, but nevertheless a spoke was put in our wheels, for our warden's man-servant, who was jealous and got across us, so I was obliged to give up either the rations or the tavern. The rations were too much for us to die and not enough to live and I could not give anything to my husband. I chose the tavern and as I had nothing to get started with, I had to go from one to another of the Christians to get them to stand surety for me, running to one to pay the other.

In this state, God blessed me miraculously for not only did I earn money for my husband and my children, but everyday I could send food and drink for six or eight men, which helped our fellow countrymen to gain a little strength. Business went so well that I had to take on two men-servants and a servant girl, which cost me quite dear. I made big profits between 24$^{th}$ June and 21$^{st}$ September, the day when my house collapsed and the King was deposed and on that same day I lost 120 ducats worth of wine and *eau de vie* in barrels and another 50 ducats through the collapse of the house.

## Moulay Muhammad II ben Arbia (1736-38)

The mother of the King fled on the 22$^{nd}$ September at first light. When the Christians noticed it, they hid her with the guard in the holes and corners near the river, since the King wanted to take her away and that is why in the night, as he was fleeing, he searched for her, but couldn't find her. And here we were again without a King and we had no news of the Christians, so that we were in the greatest anxiety in case the King had taken them away. On the fourth day, we had news that they were safe and that same day they arrived at the *bagnio*. The next day, they proclaimed Sidi Magomet Ulda Lariba[70] king; he was a good king for the Christians, but a child for the country.

**Famine and More Slaves Ransomed**

During the reign of this King, we went through a lamentable period in which life became very dear and this lasted from 1737 until June 1738; 48 000 people died of hunger, the living devoured the dead, mothers their children. There was not a dog or a cat left. The bones of cattle were dug up out of the ground and crushed between two stones and drunk with water. They ate the plaster from the walls and straw like animals, for want of grass. The King's captives received each day, instead of bread, a couple of handfuls of olives pits, from which the oil had been extracted. Food was lacking even in the royal palace, but there they did not die of hunger.

Nevertheless, from Christian lands hundreds of boats laden with wheat arrived, but this was not of much use to the Royal City, for the King and townsmen's convoys were pillaged by the country people, who were in revolt against the King, with a result that the high prices in the town of Meknès were much more serious than elsewhere. We now had to pay 2 ducats for ten pounds of wheat and one could not always get it and other foods followed in the same manner. People had no more money, but God performed a marvel for us Christians for, first of all, the King freed the Spaniards[71] in the year 1736, in the middle of November and on the 10th of August in the year 1737 at the beginning of the time of high prices, he let the French go, so that of us Dutch there remained only 28, as well as three Portuguese who, through God's goodness, had survived in spite of our enemies. We were not flourishing, without a government, as the reader will understand from what follows.

## Hard Labour

Shortly after the departure of the French, there were few Christians left, so that the Christians were forced to work more. My husband, who had always had a dispensation from the King, was forced to work with blows and violence, which was intolerable to me and I wanted to take advantage of an occasion when the King was outside his palace. I went to present myself before him with my husband and child, but could not reach him, for the King had already gone back into the palace and the gates were closed. I had decided not to go home until I had come before the King, but that had not succeeded; nevertheless I arranged to be summoned by the King with my husband and child.

So, we arrived at the palace where one of his deputies led me and my child inside and into the presence of the King and his women, where I was received with the greatest kindness and the King asked me what were my desires. I answered the King that I begged him to exempt my husband from all labour, so that he could earn his bread for me and the child, as had been the case in the time of his father and his brothers, who had been kings. The King, on learning that my husband had been set to labour without orders, was angered by this and asked me why I had not told him earlier. I told the King that after the departure of the Spaniards who had been freed, I would have come before him if I had not been prevented, for I would have asked the King to give me the house of that Spanish woman, which the King his father had bought for married Christians and had given it to them to live and have a business, for it was not fitting for married Christians to live in the *knoo* with the other Christians. That the house which the Queen had given me, had collapsed and I was now forced to lodge among the other Christians. The King responded very favourably to this and answered that he would give me a house in the town, whichever I liked best. And that my husband would not be harassed and that whoever spoke ill of me or my husband and my child could be certain of falling into disgrace with the King.

I was not a little astonished at this kind and helpful reception and the King gave me, as a slave, to one of his legitimate wives and ordered me to come every day to the palace, which I undertook to do. After having filled my hands and those of my child, the King then sent me to the town with two women, his deputies, ordering them to see that no one harassed my husband or my child.

## Maria ter Meetelen is in Favour with the King

The Governor of the town had to give me a house, the one that would please me best and in addition a *torseman*[72] that is to say a language teacher, since I still did not know the language well enough, to come with me each day before the King as interpreter. So they gave me an Irish renegade, who had turned Turk after many torments, and I chose the house of a Bashi where I went to live. The King's orders were so strict that no one dared say a bad word to us. I had to go to the royal house every day with my interpreter and sometimes I spent an hour or two with my mistress and the interpreter before the King and I told him about all sorts of rare plants and all sorts of products that came from foreign lands and I informed the King in detail about all the landscapes, kingdoms and towns that I knew very well because of my travels, which had given me a great deal of experience, and this gave the King great pleasure and day by day I was more and more well-seen by him.

Finding myself now in the King's good graces in a period of such grievously high prices, I thought of my brothers, the Christians, who were not receiving rations from the King and I asked that they should receive a dispensation from labouring for the King and this I obtained on the 14th September. The King showered beautiful clothes and linen on us, me, my husband and my child and, since my husband was now well supplied with clothing, I carried some to the other slaves in the King's palace. I had the King come out of his palace and review all the Christian slaves and dispense them from labour. The rumour that I was in such high favour with the King spread so far about the land that people from the countryside who had a complaint to make before the King came to me with gifts so that I would present their petition to the King. But God enlightened my heart and I remembered that I was a slave and I sent

*Man and Woman from North Africa – anonymous print, late 16th century.*

them to the Bashis so that they didn't get any support from me. I was required to go to the Palace every day, so I was exhausted by it and so I made out that I was sick in order to stay at home. But then for three days I had a messenger from the King asking about my health, who brought a sheep or chickens or sweetmeats from the King.

## The King's Violence against his Women

I was so seldom in my house that I stayed there for about three days; there was always mourning amongst the womenfolk in the Palace because the women there were always being beaten or strangled. So one night I was fetched by the King's bodyguard. When I came to the King's palace, the King had killed two of his concubines. He was blazing with anger and he had also punished one of his secondary wives very severely, so that my mistress was in deathly fear, and there was a black woman that he had throttled.

The King had been ten days out hunting, and had hunted a wild boar and brought it back alive, and the King had summoned me so that I could see it, and because it was so late I couldn't make it out in the dark of the night, but the King ordered me to come in the day, because then I could see that pig fighting with the dogs, which I did. Around midnight I and my interpreter and two bodyguards went back to the city, and because it was such a late hour we went out through the lesser gateway so we could go the shortest way. About half-way my interpreter broke her leg, so that she had to stay in a village on the way and I came safely home. Early the next day I went before the King to tell him [about this], and he gave me another interpreter, who was a Moorish woman born in Spain. The Bashi of Tangiers had taken her in exchange for Christian slaves. Because of the accident to my interpreter, I asked the King for a pack-mule to ride on. The previous day my mistress had been given a big costly donkey with a saddle and silver bridle and stirrups covered with red fabric as a present, so that she could ride daily with the King to his court, so the King gave me this donkey, which from that time I rode to and from the palace every day.

I immediately got on the donkey and so rode to the city.

## A Wild Boar Fight

So, in the afternoon, I went back to the King to see the wild boar fight. I had hardly been there for an hour when the King went to the arena with his wives and me, and he had brought the dogs and the wild boar. It was a terrifying beast with four tusks that could go round a human leg. There was also a black woman who deserved death. She was brought as well to fight the wild boar and thus be devoured by the dogs and the wild boar. But I obtained mercy for her and she didn't have to go into the arena. While the dogs and the wild boar were at each other's throats, The King asked me if the Christians would be glad to eat this wild boar. I said yes, but it would first have to have is throat cut. The King seeing some difficulties in getting it cut[73] said that it was not possible.

Meanwhile, the wild boar had ripped open the belly of a dog with a blow from its tusk and all its intestines came out. Another dog had broken the wild boar's leg by snapping at it and it was limping and sometimes fell down. Then I said to the King that if there were a huntsman who could very quickly throw down the animal and sit on it, I could very well slit its throat. But, as it is the custom that no man should be present, because the King's wives are not supposed to be seen by men, the above-mentioned black woman received the order to seize the wild boar, which she did. She was as black as ink, but once in the arena she became as white as snow because of the fear that seized her. She had quite a fight to hold on to it until I got down. I had my child on my arm, who was twenty-one months[74] old and I fastened it on my back so as to be able to run away better. Then I went and sat next to the black woman on the wild boar and I cut his throat, but not without great danger, for if we had not been quick enough, he could still very well have thrown us down and attacked us. The wild boar continued to walk with his throat cut until he fell down. I and the black woman then came back to the King and his wives who were not a little afraid, for they had repeatedly shouted at me to get out of there. He said to me:

"*Hola, entaa rosel bel rosel lagor.*"[75]

## Famine, Cannibalism and the Fate of the *Mellah*

During this time, the cost of living continued to increase and nothing was delivered, either for the King or his subjects and we lived through a very difficult and devastating period. For winter was approaching and there were no crops in the fields or on the trees, with the result that there was no food at all, either for men or beasts, so that in the country beasts ate each other and men ate men. The roads and paths that I used every day were strewn with corpses. They died in such numbers that they could not even bury them. In the graveyards, the dead were piled up as high as a man and they could not put them in the earth. The houses remained empty and they stripped the shops of their doors and their wood. The dead lay, some half eaten, others completely, and so it went on and these were the most dreadful times.

The Jews who lived outside the city between the walls and a gate were composed of about 1400 households that lived there. They too died in such numbers that it was impossible to bury their dead according to their custom, that is to say to wash them and sew them in a white linen cloth and lay them with solemnity in the earth. They stuffed their dead under the ruins of old collapsed houses. Of these fourteen hundred households, not even two hundred remain. One would have said it was the destruction of Jerusalem. It is impossible to describe what I saw and heard daily. We could not buy the smallest thing in the market without immediately being surrounded by starving people, who watched us like a lion its prey. If they could have, they would have robbed us and fled away eating as they went. It is impossible to describe or relate with the tongues of men what happened during that terrible time of high prices and famine. In the meadows, the fields and the mountains one found people who had died of hunger, who had gone out there to look for grass roots and weeds to fill their empty stomachs.

The King, seeing the misery of his people, was moved by pity, with the result that the taxes were slightly lowered. And as the country people were in revolt, one group against another, it was also impossible to have provisions brought from there, and as a result the King decided to free all the Christians, if only someone would come and fetch them. It was impossible to write from the town to the Noble Lords of the States, since all the mail was looted. At this point, the King wanted to send my husband with a convoy of Bashis to Tangiers[76]. From there, they would send an Ambassador on the advice of a Jew called Rabi ben Queque whose brother had been here in Holland[77] to negotiate with Their High Lordships over the buying back of slaves, in accordance with what he had advised the King.

My husband did not much want to leave alone with the Bashi and the Jew without having other Christians with him and the King would not have allowed that if I had not explained it to the King. There was also a man from Hamburg who had already come to an agreement with the Jew and had promised him ten ducats if he would claim him back from the King, but the Jew's wings were too short: he did not obtain this.

The day of my husband's departure arrived. My husband received his passport from the King to set out on the following day. The man from Hamburg, seeing that he had no chance of leaving with him, incited my husband against me saying that it was my fault, which put me in such a rage that I immediately saddled my donkey and went to the palace to see the King and I asked him to give my husband one more travelling companion. He agreed at once and sent me to his scribe to change the passport and add the name of the one I had chosen. The clerk having written the passport, I went to take it to the King, who set his seal on it. And so I brought it back to the house and all matters were resolved.

They set out on the 5th November, 1737. On the 10th of the same month, they arrived at Tangiers and went to the Bashi, who sent them to the *bagnio*. He put them in irons with a chain round their neck by way of welcome, but they did not stay there long, for they bought themselves out with their money, twenty gold ducats, and so they were set free again. Then they went to Tétouan where they stayed until the Jew set out with them at the end of March for Salé, where Captain Joost Sels[78], came with his ship to negotiate for the freeing of slaves, which we will speak of later in more detail.

## Brigands and Other Dangers

Scarcely had my husband left than I asked the King to grant me rations and he made me an allowance at the same rate as his legitimate wives – four pounds of wheat per day. I had a Jewish woman in my service as well as a Christian man. I sent away my woman servant and asked the King to let me have about four Christians, because I lived in town and it was a little dangerous to live there in those times of high prices. and in this way my house would be protected from all the evil-doers, given that all anyone did was steal and pillage. The King gave me permission to choose as many Christians out of the pack [as I wanted] and this I did. I got them food and clothes.

I went on going to the royal palace every day and attending all the entertainments with the King and his women and walking every day in the courtyards. Sometimes I stayed the whole night with my child, who was much loved by the King, more than his own child. It was very dangerous to go into the town in the evening, because of the brigands. The King, on learning there were so many bandits in the palace and its surroundings, who sometimes stole the King's food in broad daylight and even in his house, gave me a pistol with powder and balls and also a sabre, with orders to kill anyone who accosted me in order to steal.

So, every day I set out for the palace with one of my Christians with a loaded gun behind me and another with a saber before me. One evening, not long after, I received an order from the King to come to the palace. On the way, I met with bandits who were hiding behind some little hillocks. When we saw them, we immediately fired on them and they took good care not to get near us. But I never heard any more from them, so I could easily go to the royal palace at night without being harassed, something that the King's people could not do. Although, they beat the dogs for barking, barking dogs don't bite. A soldier from our country can take on three of them, because they are terribly cowardly, but with a wounded man they are stout fellows.

**Maria ter Meetelen defends her Mistress**

The affection of the King for me grew daily, which was a wonderful exercise of God's authority for the protection of our slaves, who otherwise might possibly have been led to slaughter in order to fill their empty stomachs. Because if the King wished the Christians well, his people would not do them wrong. I had so much influence over the King that when I was present he never said a rude word to his wives. So it happened one day that I had come to the palace and the King didn't know of it. The King called my mistress and asked for the special one who had not yet come, whereupon the King became so enraged that he hit his wife, my good mistress. I in my chamber hearing this at once sprang up and rescued my mistress, whom the King left forthwith without saying a word. He went away like a dog who has been whipped. Having taken my mistress to her room and secured her there, I followed the King to where he had gone, and sent one ahead with the matter, whereupon I soon put myself forward.

The King seeing that I had so followed him and inquired, and this diminishing his anger that he should have done something that I had prevented [him from doing][79], went to an upstairs room in his palace with a few of his wives. Shortly afterwards I dispatched my interpreter with one of his concubines [to deal with] with the matter and I charged my interpreter that she must not go before the King, but should stand behind the door listening to what the King said, where she stayed a few hours, whereupon a messenger came from the King [telling me] that I must go to the King. I asked her whether I should go alone without my interpreter and she said yes, whereupon I was afraid because I knew how things stood and I thought now I shall now be held to account for my forwardness. But I took courage and thought: I can only die one death. I sent my mistress to her chamber and then went to the King, who spoke to me in a friendly way.

## Lectures on Astrology and Whales

The King being curious about all the arts and sciences, and I, having crept through the world and knowing something of everything, gave an account of everything, such as astrology, which is why the King tendered me two globes: a heavenly sphere and the earth, which we dealt with daily. And so we proceeded with the whales, and where they could be caught, and in what manner, and how big they were, and of more such sea creatures in Greenland, which gave the King great pleasure. Meanwhile I took the opportunity to reconcile him with my mistress, which was accomplished before midnight, and the King leaving for his bath said to me also to come there with my mistress; it did not seem right and I delayed. My interpreter, who I had found to be false, I left where she was and I said to the King that she was looking after my child. By then I already knew the Turkish language well, so that I could manage very well without her.

## The Queen Restored to Favour

My interpreter, who came to me with nothing but rags and was now a notable lady, sought with falsehood to bring me into disfavour with the King. I came to see this because she was close to the head wife of the King, who was so hostile towards me that she would have poisoned me if she could. But the fox was too sly for her, which is why she contrived with my interpreter, because my mistress was always in the King's favour, and whenever she fell out of favour, I was the go-between. The King caught on to this and put his head wife in prison, where she stayed for three months. My interpreter was forbidden to come to the palace and the King burdened me with with my former interpreter, the renegade, whom I immediately brought with me, but how the King came to know of the business I never discovered. After three months had gone by it was the Easter[80] of the King and then it is the custom that the closest friends of the King come and wish the King many blessings for Easter. So the sisters of his head wife also came to wish the King Happy Easter and to seek pardon for their sister, which they got. She was taken out of the prison and brought before the King, who gave her back her queenly robes and jewelry, as [it] is the custom there if someone falls into disfavour with the King, that everything is taken away from her and she is put naked into an apartment within the house. She gets no more than one slave to feed her, if she has rich friends they must put something by for her. Shortly after she had come out of prison she took occasion with me because I was so true to my mistress and didn't want to do anything for her, whereupon I answered: "Two hats don't belong on one head." And that the King had given me to my mistress, that I would put my life in the balance for her and that I couldn't do that for another, whereupon she was furious and complained of me to the King, but she was judged wrong and I right. Upon which she almost burst open with rage and she couldn't do anything because I walked upright so that I dreaded no one before God.

## A Strange Theft Angers the Christian Community

In the meantime something happened that stirred up quite a commotion among our people. There were a few troublemakers who were working to make themselves master over all our people and make them submissive. To which end they had bribed the [King's] attendant so that with her help they could come to the King, where they would seemingly go to ask for bread. And then the King's attendant would try to get the King to hand over to these troublemakers the means with which our people earned their bread, [by] shutting down the tavern owners who were married. A few of our people who had caught wind of it told me and asked for my advice. I told them they should keep quiet, that I would take care of the matter, which I did. Because I made it known to the King and told him that they would come before the King to ask for bread, and I advised the King not to answer them, which fortunately was what happened so that they didn't come to the Court of the King, so their effort was all for nothing.

But they made out that they had come upon money [held] by our people, as if they had broken through a wall that was an ell thick and wide, and broken open a chest that was remarkably strong and heavy, and cleaned the money out of it and set off with it, but they were caught and put in prison.[81] The people were so embittered by this that they sought their lives, to which end they asked me to go before the King and ask the King to hand out justice to these two prisoners as was the custom and use of our land, and that was to hang them. And that they had a letter signed by all the people, that when our ambassador came this would be paid back with the rest.

The King should have agreed to it if they had indeed come before the King, but I had anticipated all this, so that they couldn't carry on any business with the King without me. I was then put under pressure to carry it through, but I didn't, because they had half of the money back again, and moreover I knew very well what would follow. For which reason I thought through the business by myself and on my own authority said that I had spoken to the King about it and that the King took the position that they be punished but that they must take care to give them no ordeal that would cause them injury or they would be repaid in kind. The news was very unwelcome, because they were like snorting lions and wanted to make me suffer for it.

**One of the Thieves Converts**

They said that I was on the side of the thieves, so that I had to plead [my case] against twenty-two men, and that I was [acting] alone. Meanwhile in the evening the miscreants were brought before all our people, who were gathered there. I had to make an appearance with them, although I would much rather have stayed at home. I was then asked if the ones who initiated such crimes didn't deserve to be punished. I answered yes, but they must take into account that we were the King's slaves, and they must deal moderately with them, but it was like throwing oil onto the fire. I went quickly from that place to my house in the city, and they went to punish the distressed pair and set them apart in separate prisons. And in the night one of them broke open the door and fled hell for leather to the Turkish church[82] and became a Turk.

The day had hardly broken when I had the head of our people at my house, with the attendant who took my report of it, and they compelled me to go to the King, which was necessary because of the one in the hands of the Moors. And if the Moors came before the King with it, they would have placed many complaints against the Christians, and that would have been disastrous for all of us. I sped my way to the King and they all followed me, with the miscreants [sic] and the attendant and a few of the head people, who wanted to influence the heaviness of the complaints, but I was well on my guard. I then came before the King and presented it to him in the best possible way. That it had happened out of the distress of hunger, and that the King well knew in what difficult times we lived, and that the punishment of God was enough, punishments we couldn't avert, with many of the circumstances. And I beseeched the King that they wouldn't suffer any harm and that the King would only allow the miscreants to come before him, which was what had so embittered my brothers, and that they would only make the King's head warm with complaining.

The King thought my request was fit, and agreed that I bring the two miscreants before him, who I then had brought in. And they thought to go in with them, but when they heard that the King wanted to have no one [else] before him, they were angrier still. I then brought both miscreants before the King, and the Christian fell at the feet of the King and begged for his life and the King pardoned him and the other made his profession of the Turkish faith, and was sent to the Governor of the city to be circumcised. And I went back inside again with the King, who made twenty times apologies that it was not his fault that the Christian had become a Turk. Because the King had asked him if it was from fear, that nothing bad would happen to him, and that he could stay a Christian.

## The Christians Plot against Maria ter Meetelen

I then went to my house where I was made to suffer for it, even by those who I had given food to in that difficult time, but they didn't dare to do me any harm. But they went away and tried by means of the attendant to strangle me in my house, for which purpose she bribed one of the King's bodyguards and a female black slave, a *gesantinne*[83] of the King. These were meant to strangle me in my house in the name of the King, but it went wrong. They were scared that the attendant would betray them, so they took on the servant of the attendant to help them take the attendant's life, and then his servant would appeal to the King.

The servant doing his best served them well, so that one day he removed a letter from his master's bedroom, that the attendant of King Muly Abdela had received that was very hostile about the reigning King, so that it would have cost him his life if it came into the hands of the King. He brought me the letter with a piece of eight, and made me swear I would deliver the letter to the present King, which I duly swore. I let this be read by a *renegado*'s son, so I would know the contents, which I immediately disclosed to the attendant, who at once fled to the church, because he knew it would cost him his head. I took it with me to the palace and had a hard struggle to hand it over to the King. I resolved that I would give the King something else in its place so that I could blind the eyes of my interpreter, since I didn't trust her. I worked it so adroitly that my interpreter had no idea whether I had delivered the letter to the King or not, which she also confirmed to the Christians when we returned. Meanwhile late in the evening while they all lay sleeping, I went to my office to write a letter to my husband and burnt the letter to ashes because I was afraid they would go through my papers.

The attendant, seeing that King didn't ask him any questions and that there was no declaration about it, appeared again outside the church, which made our people very discontented, but they were powerless. Meanwhile, I had done my best with the King in this long distressing time so that fourteen of those that I thought the most needy received bread from the King, which had again caused great division among them, for those around the ones that had the free food also wanted to have it, and it was with the greatest difficulty that I had secured it from the King.

The King's slaves or prisoners must foul themselves daily for a few handfuls of olive pits, and could not get anything else, so that they had to buy bread every day from the Christians, who were too spoilt to eat the bread made from barley flour, from which it can be seen what they were in want of. The suffering that I and my people underwent in the reign of Sidi Magomet Ulda Lariba could not be described, and after the King was deposed it was even worse, but those who can suffer and endure win, their enemies defeated. They suffered all manner of tricks and lies, but I couldn't bring this up before the King and his circle, because the King's fondness for me was too great, as was also that of his whole family and all the great ones of the city, including the Bashis and the governors, who respected me, yes, until the last hour I was in Turkey. Because I walked upright with them and therefore they trusted me like the gospel. And where I could take a stone out of the path, I did so for peace and prosperity, as much for the Turks as for the Christians.

## Debate on Astrology

Meanwhile every day I was with the King philosophising vigorously about astrology, about which I had so great a command of learning that he considered me the greatest scholar in his whole country. So that he made it known to some of his greatest and foremost men, to come to me and discourse with me about astrology. And a Jewish rabbi - they were then more esteemed than the Turks in religious doctrine - was also summoned by the King. It was on 8th April, 1738 that eight of the King's scholars and the Jewish rabbi gathered before the King where I should dispute with them regarding the passage of the sun and the moon and the stars and the movement of the whole earth, which I did plainly as God made me[84].

The King, sharper in comprehension than them all, understood the matter and they knew better than to disprove it. Excusing themselves, they said it went against their faith, but the King gave them the answer, that it wasn't spoken against their faith, but they should simply say: "We don't understand it". They went away shamefaced.

**The Dutch Ambassador**

Meanwhile our Ambassador, so long awaited, arrived: Captain Joos Sels, with whom the King entered into negotiations, but they could not come to an agreement, for the King wanted the money that was supposed to be given for himself and on the other hand, the Blacks also wanted this money, so the arrangement would not work. And the King asked for nothing better than to free us, but he did not know how to get hold of the money, and he consulted me often, but I could not see any way, for the King depended on the Blacks and every year their received their *retep*[85] or salary from the King, but the King's treasury was empty, so the King hesitated over what it would be best for him to do. The King then resolved to give me and my husband and our children our freedom[86], as well as some precious objects as gifts, that is to say some tiger[87] skins and lions and fine carpets and silken clothing and handkerchiefs, the like of which one rarely sees in Europe.

And this would have happened if there had not been spies who carried everything back to the Blacks, so that the most faithful friend of the King, the Governor of Salé was discharged from his position and replaced by another because of the Blacks. He then arrived in the town to discuss the question of our freedom with our countrymen, to obtain which he would be given two hundred ducats that the Fathers would then pay him. This Governor persuaded the King so effectively that he resolved to send us away and give the money to the Blacks who were on campaign with their army with a view to an expedition with the King. At two o'clock, he was in the town. And that same day, the 22nd June, they published an order saying that anyone who wanted to buy wheat could go to the army to buy it or carry it away and it would not then cost more than two *dubbeltjes* for a ten pound measure, while that same day it had cost 60 *dubbeltjes*.

## The King Deposed

That same evening, I went to the King to describe all this to him and to get him to put his seal on the passport, so that we could get ready to leave on the following day. The King, who was not in a good mood, ordered me to come back in the morning and I got ready to go there again on the following morning but my interpreter, on going out, was almost stripped, but escaped, for the King had been made prisoner at midnight and put in irons and we found ourselves again without a King. I had to leave our house in haste and go back to the house I had in the *bagnio*.

I had scarcely entered when I was again insulted by the Christians who wanted to accuse me to the Blacks of having quantities of precious stones and gold from the King and they made my life impossible, in revenge for the good days in the past. But he who hunts another can never stand still, and so it was with them[88]. And that is what happened to them. I was never free of being harassed, with the result that I was obliged to leave my house and place myself under the protection of a Bashi, to whose house I went with a present and my two children and asked to remain under his protection until a king came, because my brother Christians were making me suffer greatly. I told all this to the Bashi and he promised his protection until the coming of the King. I only stayed there for two days and a night when the Bashi arranged things so that I could go home peacefully and without fear.

Meanwhile the Jews, having learned that our people had promised two hundred ducats to obtain their freedom, spoke to some of the youngest of our nation, who did not understand what this country was like and they made them fine speeches, promising them freedom, if they could help them to find a few hundred ducats to give as a present to the chief Bashi of the Blacks. All this was to be done before the arrival of the King, since the King once more had to be fetched from afar and this could take another good month and by then we could already be free. But, alas, we were very far from that and a sad new slavery awaited us as the honoured reader will see further ahead. I knew this very well, but there was nothing I could say and with what these gentlemen put forward, I had to agree.

## Accusations Against Maria ter Meetelen

So, we left Meknès on the 2nd of July and reached Mammora[89], which is a seaport near Salé, on the 5th and there I found my husband and his companion who bade me welcome, as well as our compatriots, who thanked them with great joy. We were given tents to spend the night, but when the merchants learned of all the troubles that our fellow countrymen made us suffer daily, they lodged us – me, my husband and my children, with the Governor's permission. But they tried harder and harder to torment us, so they incited the Jew who had brought them there against me and he summoned me. I, unaware of everything, went and he treated me very badly and demanded that I give him money. The more I said that I had nothing, the more he overwhelmed me with insults and hurtful words and said that every day I had received two ducats from the King, as well as a large quantity of jewels, which was a vulgar lie. He threatened me saying that he would surely arrange things so as to get this money out of me, which he put into effect not long after. Captain Sels was anchored before the Bay of Mammora and was negotiating with the merchants and the Jew for our freedom, but they could not reach an agreement.

While this was going on, from time to time the Jew had to travel to Romel[90], to the Blacks' camp, a short day's journey from Mammora, to report to the head Bashi and to make a report about the negotiations with the Ambassador or Captain Sels. In the Bashi's house, there was a Jewish woman who had turned Turk and roused against us by the Jew, she was supposed to ask the Bashi's wives to see the Christian woman - that was me. It was granted them by the Bashi that I should be brought, which suited the Jew, as he wanted to torment me. So they came to Mammora, giving themselves a great deal of importance, as if I was going to be burned at once or torn apart. I knew well what it was about, for they were searching my place for money - and as there wasn't any, they were searching by force [sic]. If I had had money, I would gladly have given it in order to be free of all these troubles, but give a sheep today and tomorrow they will be back for a cow and they will not leave you in peace until they have sucked you dry. I offered them everything I had in this world and said I would go back to my country naked and bare, but it was in vain. He said that if I did not give it to him willingly, the Bashi would take it from me anyway.

Early in the morning they took us, my husband, my children and me, to the Bashi and we were accompanied by some of our countrymen who were jubilant:

"Now the King's whore will be burnt. If she doesn't want to give money and jewels, burn her, burn her, burn her."

And one of them spat after me. I remained patient and thought:

"God will avenge me!"

And indeed later they met their retribution at home[91]. That is why he who can suffer and endure finds his enemies defeated. So, in the afternoon we arrived before the Bashi and my husband stayed with our things and with the animals, and me and my children were taken to the Bashi and his women, who received me very kindly and hoped that God would soon hasten my deliverance. I thanked the Bashi for this and he sent me to his wife around whom were all the wives sent by the important people to see me and they were all very friendly towards me and nothing they said gave me any pain and they gave me food and drink.

Meanwhile, this converted Jewess came to me and said in Spanish:

"Tell me where you have put the money and jewels. Your husband has already confessed and they have punished him severely and now are busy skinning him alive and if you don't tell me, they will come immediately and fetch you to do the same to you."

When I heard these words, a terrible grief assailed my heart, so that I could hardly say a word and tears streamed from my eyes. When I answered, it was as follows:

"Oh! Leave my husband alone, he is as innocent as my child and let me die in his place. All the same, I have nothing."

And then I could not go on speaking.

I stayed sitting like that for several hours, with my children on my lap weeping bitterly with me and this Jewess came back with new lamentations, causing me new vexations, so that it seemed that my husband was already dead. Then I came to myself again somewhat and prepared to die and entrusted my children to the hand of the Lord and thought of the way in which God had already saved me from innumerable dangers, and had been my Father and my Mother, from the age of thirteen, and had always taken care of me. And I said:

"Oh, God! You are always this same God and I know that nothing happens without Your knowledge and You arrange everything for the best and that if You come to take away my children, Lord, You will be their Father and Protector. I commend them to Your care."

And I comforted myself with God and took courage, and I was ready to die and I tried to find a way to come before the Bashi and prove my husband innocent, but they stopped me. Towards evening this converted

Jewess came back and said that now I would be taken before the Bashi, but I had to cry hard when I was there; then I noted the falsity of this female creature and I went before the Bashi who received me no less kindly than before and treated me with a great deal of respect, as if I were not a slave.

Meanwhile, my husband had also come and was speaking to the Bashi. Turning round, I saw that no harm had come to him. I was as if reborn and my heart rejoiced. And after having taken leave of the Bashi, who wished me all kinds of blessings and freedom, and told me that he hoped to come to an agreement with our Ambassador, we went to the place where they took us to spend the night. And I asked my husband whether anyone had maltreated him, but no one had spoken to him, for either good or bad.

The Jew could not stay still and since the expenses of the Moor were still to be paid, he began to torment me again. I had a bag in which were my clothes and those of my husband and of my children and I emptied it and said:

"That is all I possess in the world."

But finding nothing there that pleased him, he lost interest and then it was necessary to hand over the little bit of money that the Consul of Cadix [Cadiz] had sent us and so my countrymen lost it through their own fault.

## The Reign of Moulay al-Mustadi.

At the end of four days, we were brought back to Mammora. Our countrymen had not expected anything but our execution and were stupefied. We did not stay for long, for on August 4$^{th}$ the King made his entry into the palace as king; he immediately recalled all the Christians and sent the necessary number of mules to fetch us. We, who had thought to be freed, returned with nothing to a new slavery and when we arrived on August 21$^{st}$, found that in our absence we had been stripped of what we had left there by three Portuguese who had stayed behind. We were given back our beds, a table and some little benches and that was all.

### Winemaking

On the 22$^{nd}$ of the same month, we were taken before the King who gave each of us Christians a modest little place in the palace to guard the warehouse and he set us to work, but my husband was dispensed from labour. So, we had nothing to allow us to eat, nor anything to enable us to start doing something. I, therefore, had to set to work, if I didn't want to die of hunger together with my husband and children, and that year there was a good grape harvest, but money was lacking. Now the merchants of Salé had arrived with a present for the King on his accession to the throne and I had a great deal of trouble getting a loan from them of 20 ducats to do my *Vendimi* or wine harvest. We got the grapes cheap and only paid 12 to 14 *stuyvers* for 100 pounds. So my husband harvested the grapes to get some money and soon provided the tavern with sparkling wine and *eau de vie*, obtained by distilling the grapes, so that at the end of 8 or 10 days we were once again in a position to earn our bread.

Our tavern was outside our living quarters; by night a Christian, who worked during the daytime in the King's warehouse, inhabited it and in the daytime my husband was there. It had scarcely been got up and running when my husband caught a very serious disease of the eyes, which laid him up for a good two months, so that the tavern had to close, which did not rejoice my heart, for during this time I would still have been able to earn something before the King went back to the army. Furthermore, my children too were very unwell and I could only see out of one eye and the King's Fast[92] was about to begin soon when it was forbidden to sell spirits and my husband did not want to go to our tavern. I turned to others to persuade him to let me go there with all my people. I had to make do with very little because there was only very little space – so, I dealt with everything: housework and tavern, and God gave me great strength and blessed me very greatly in my business. In one month, I earned enough to make us as much wine and *eau de vie* as I had made before. We could put enough aside, in addition to feeding ourselves during Lent and at last I could, once more, reckon my capital at a hundred ducats.

The Christians then left me in peace for a little, but not for long. For when they came back from the army with the King they did everything possible to take the tavern away from me or to forbid me it, so that every day I had new and serious troubles. I was still not too sure whether the King was benevolent towards the Christians or not, and I decided to take a chance and go before him to ask him to let me have a house in the town to keep a tavern. I pleased the King by the petition I presented to him; he showed his pleasure by granting me what I asked. But the Moors and the Bashis advised him against it; they considered it was somewhat dangerous in the town for my household all alone and that having my house in the *bagnio* I could keep the tavern, but my brothers

*Bab Berdame – postcard c.1920.*

– i.e. Christians - were opposed to it and stopped me. I had not done anything wrong and did not say anything about it to the King, for otherwise they would have paid dearly.

The King told me to go to the *bagnio* with my husband and children and that if anyone tried to stop me, all I had to do was come and complain to him and he would cut off their heads. So I went back and continued keeping my tavern, but the others did not stop doing everything possible to harm us, my husband and me. So I looked for an opportunity to go to the King's mother and I managed without too much trouble to go there every day and also to his sister, whose affection for me became so great that I could get everything I wanted from her and never came back with empty hands, but sometimes I brought a bag of flour, or meat, or money or fruit and I was the favourite of all the royal family.

## The Third Reign of Moulay Abdallah (1740-41)

### Moulay al-Mustadi Deposed

Now it so happened that the King had already been king for a year and we could not foresee that the King was going to be deposed. I had gone early in the morning to the palace and at five o'clock in the afternoon a messenger arrived announcing that another King had been proclaimed and that the Blacks were in front of the palace to capture this King, but nevertheless he was able to escape. When I learned this news, I took my leave of the Queen Mother and the sister of the King, which did not take place without the shedding of tears on one side and the other. And I comforted them saying that it was the will of God that it should be so and they believed it firmly and gave me a little money for the last time. I had scarcely gone out of the door of the house when I saw everyone in the streets crying very loudly:

"Long life to Muly Abdela!"

And I, who was neither sleeping nor dozing, realized at once how dangerous this was for me and cried at the top of my voice:

"Long life to Muly Abdela!"

However, a Moor said to me:

"Why do you cry long life to Muly Abdela for you have just come from the mother of the deposed king. You like him more than Muly Abdela."

I answered him briefly and adroitly and asked if he was well aware that kings were proclaimed and kings were deposed, and that I recognized the one who had been proclaimed king, and that I wanted to be his slave, and that Muly Abdela had been good to me, to my husband and my children. The Moor, quite satisfied, let me go away in peace and so I went through the palace to the town in the middle of cries of joy:

"Long life to Muly Abdela!"

Meanwhile, my husband who was in town was very worried and the guard was already imagining, given my delay, that I might have been arrested and imprisoned, as I had indeed run the risk of being. For when a king is driven out, it is the same for all his servants and they flee in all directions to escape and not be captured. For this reason the guard had left his post and gone to the palace. We met up under the outer gate and, very worried, he said to me:

"Maria, aren't you afraid?" A new king has been proclaimed and you are still inside the palace, it's a miracle that they haven't arrested you."

Then I told him how I had crossed the palace shouting: "Long life to Muly Abdela!" and what had happened to me.

The guard, on hearing this, was just as surprised as pleased. Then I crossed the town to go to my house to the great astonishment of all the Moors I met on my way, who asked me if the deposed king really had been deposed.

So, I arrived at my house, which I found full of sadness and mourning, but when they saw me back again with my child, the joy was all the greater. A few days after, the mother of the King arrived at the palace to take charge of the kingdom until the arrival of her son. I went at once to present my congratulations to the throne. I found my old mistress, the mother of the King, who had been driven out, and her daughter. They were there, treated like evil-doers, to turn over whatever they had belonging to the kingdom to the Queen Regent. They were stripped of everything and sent to another palace belonging to the previous king, where all the women of the previous king were sent as well.

They were given fixed rations, as we do here to the crew of our national fleet, of butter, cheese and lard, but they got much less. Their rations consisted of only two and half pounds of flour and only those who had some land from which they could get supplies could manage. It was really very little, so that it was too much to die, but too little to live. I then delivered my respects to the new Queen, but it was not as pleasant as with the old, so that I neglected to go back there, as I was not sufficiently welcome.

The King arrived soon after and at once summoned all the Christians, whom he immediately set to work. To our absolute delight, my husband was again sent to the warehouse, while the others were forced to march for at least an hour outside the town to go to their work, since the King had installed a camp outside the town, where he had set up his tents with his people, since he had no faith in the Blacks and did not dare live in the palace. The Blacks forced him to go and live in the palace and finally he made up his mind to it, but nevertheless he kept his tents in the country to be able to flee at any moment, for he understood perfectly well what the Blacks wanted, but the fox was too cunning for them. He was called Muly Abdela *diep*, which means "Muly the fox"[93] and this name suited him very well, for he was wilier than the foxes.

He was the best king of all for the country, but the Christians were forced to labour very hard and he took good care that they did not get better bread than under the other kings. He was a great tyrant towards his subjects, for he boasted that during his first two reigns he had had 14 000 people killed. Now, he was king for the third time, but only for four months and then he only saved his life by fleeing, for he went to Fez where he had already sent his mother earlier.

## Moulay Zayn al-'Abidīn (1741)

### Yet Another King – the Christians Forced to Move to Fez

And now once more they proclaimed yet another king, who was called Muly Sinlebdi[94]. A peasant from the country would have been more capable of ruling than this king. We didn't keep him long, for he again had to escape by fleeing, which happened at the end of four months. He was a miserable mangy jackal, who tried to rob the Christians and the Jews and the Moors; so we were not exactly sad when his reign came to an end.

## The Fourth Reign of Moulay Abdallah (1741-42)

Muly Abdela became king for the fourth time in the month of December in the year 1741 and he fixed his residence at Fez[95]. He gave orders to all the Christians great and small, without exception, to go there, which caused us great grief, since in Meknès we had our houses, our household goods, crockery, pots, winepresses and distilleries, and other utensils. All this had to stay behind as prey for the Turks, since we could not take anything with us and we were to be in a state worse than a new enslavement. This news reached us a good three days before the official confirmation.

My husband was so upset by it that he could neither eat nor drink and it was the same with many of the others. I was there with two children whom I have been able to bring back home safely. I was sad too, but nevertheless, it did not affect me as much as them. I prepared for the journey and thought: I will get well organized, so as to have both food and drink. I went to the hen house, took half a dozen hens whose throats I cut and I prepared them, together with other food and belongings, while the others, their heads sunk in their pillows, could not manage to say a word, and I insulted them a little for being such useless fellows. I counted on the wheel of fortune turning. I did not get too worried, because nothing more could happen to us except death; but I was a wise woman and I alone had a little understanding. But they saw everything in the blackest colour and were not as lacking in anxiety as I, who let everything go where the wind chose to take it.

On the third day, the categoric order arrived from the King that I was to stay there with my children, while the other Christians had to go to Fez. Everyone was plunged back into sadness and especially my husband, because I was going to have all the responsibility for all the goods of our fellow-countrymen. And their business continued to be carried on by the Jews, who were to be accountable to me, while I busied myself with my own trade.

Meanwhile, the day of their departure was fixed and I begged the guard, by promising a good reward, to do his best to get the King to free my husband, which he promised me and indeed did. As soon as the Christians arrived at Fez, the King reviewed them as much as three times and each time the guard recommended my husband to the King, but he found himself with the answer that if he insisted any more about the Christian, he would get a ball in him, at which point, the guard did not dare to insist any further.

A full month having passed, the rumour went around that the King would be deposed again, which caused me no little sorrow, because I was well aware that my husband could not save his life by fleeing because he was too fat. The others were light and could run away at night and get to Meknès, which was only a short day's journey. One allows roughly twelve hours for that. While waiting, I did not remain idle. Each time

I sent them a load of food and drink, I informed them of the King's situation, being better placed than they to know it, so that they could seek an opportunity to come back to Meknès. During this time the King, having a sense that he would not be king for much longer, summoned my husband who immediately came before him in the tent where he was lying, and asked him if he was a Christian and if he was married and if he had children and if they were boys or girls and what they were called. When my husband answered with the truth, the King asked where his wife was. He said at Meknès and he asked who was looking after her there. He said:

"The Lord."

This answered satisfied the King and he said:

"It is a sin according to my faith and yours and that of the Jews that the husband should be here and his wife elsewhere. I will send you to your wife and you will remain there until I send you away at your liberation and you will keep a tavern there for your wife and children."

Now these were very comforting and unexpected words. The King immediately gave the order to the Bashi to send my husband to Meknès and he ordered the governor to take good care of him, so that no ill should befall him and no one was to harass him to make him give something, as was the custom of the country. I could not do otherwise than give a present to the Bashi, for similar occasions could arise again and if I had not rewarded these people sufficiently, they could harm me very much more. This took place on the fortieth day after my husband's departure, when he arrived unexpectedly at the house early on Tuesday morning. Immediately a crowd of Moors surrounded my house; they considered it a miracle that the King had freed my husband, so that our guard cried very loudly:

"Maria, you are surely much loved by the King, for I went to a great deal of trouble and the King wanted to shoot me."

Eight days later, the king was deposed again. The Christians fled secretly for near him they were in great danger and Muly Mestadie[96] was again proclaimed king for the second time.

## Moulay al-Mustadi Proclaimed King Again

I did not waste any time and went again to the palace to present my congratulations to the mother of the King on the occasion of her son's ascending the throne. I was in fact received very kindly and did not come home with empty hands. The feeling of friendship towards me on the part of the mother of the King and his sister, and even the King himself increased day by day, so that I had a good influence on them and I did what I could to obtain our liberation and that of our brothers. The King did not seem opposed to it and sought a way to send me, as well as my husband and my two children, to his brother who was viceroy at Marrakech, until the arrival of an ambassador at Santa-Cruys [Agadir], in order to send me, as well as my husband children, away to freedom, because he did not know how much more time he would remain king and then the Christians would have to go back to the warehouses and if we were with his brother we would be safe.

The day of our departure was already fixed and our bags packed, but my husband was not at all happy at the idea of this journey that would last a good month to a distant place with two children in the sweltering heat, with the result that I was obliged to ask the King for permission to remain, to which he agreed. The mother and the sister of the King often insisted very vehemently that I should turn Turk and that it was a great sin that I was an unbeliever, but I always answered them that it had not yet pleased heaven and I kissed the ground before her [sic]. And when they saw they would not win me over, they asked me to raise my little girl, who was not a year old, for the son of her son, to which I replied that if that was what was to happen, I could not oppose it. That satisfied them fully and from then on they never called my daughter anything but: *la rossa ta sidi Magomet*[97], that is to say the fiancée of Sidi Magomet. That was the name of the son of the King.

I did not get at all upset about this business because I was persuaded that God would deliver me from their hands, which I do not want to tell here, having my own reasons for it. I did not tell my husband everything that happened to me with the King and his mother and sister, for he might well have stopped me going to the palace, for he did not like the Moors because they had made him suffer a great deal before my arrival in Barbary.

**Plague**

Meanwhile the plague broke out on the 13th of June in the year 1742. Every day it killed 100 people or more. The King went into the countryside with his army [and stayed] under the tent which they set up there and he

*Bab Dar al-Makhzen – postcard c.1910.*

forbade anyone of his army and the Christians who were there with him to go into the town. But these last went there in secret. The people were not free with the result that the plague was very grave, but what is most remarkable is that we Christians traded daily with the Moors and every day we were obliged to cross the town to buy food and we lived in the heart of the town. Jews and Moors were our suppliers; now they died of plague, but not one of us Christians fell ill. I had permission to go to the palace with my servant, a Jewish woman, and when I was thus crossing the town, the Moors asked me whether the plague was raging among us too. I said no. Then they asked me what to do to avoid it. I said we had no advice to give them, but it depended on what God sent us and for which they praised His glory. But then some among them said that we were unbelievers and so Muly Magomet [Muhammad] and He [God] did not know us but he did know them and therefore Magomet had sent them these hardships on this earth[98].

Our Christians were very sad and distressed, for they were afraid of catching the plague and dying; I, on the other hand, was full of courage and I firmly hoped to be freed by the end of the year, which caused several of them to jeer at me. I continued to speak of our liberation. They tired me so much that I was on the point of weakening. But in this sad crisis, I took my Bible in my hands, where I always found my salvation and my comfort[99]. Opening my Bible, I immediately found consolation there on reading it, for at the first attempt, I found these words:

"A thousand and ten thousand will fall at your left hand and at your right hand I will guard you."[100]

I rose from where I was sitting and I said:

"Whom will you fear more than God? Does not everything come from God, both life and death? Read in His word and you will find this there: a thousand and ten thousand will fall at your left hand and God will guard us at His right hand. Every day you see hundreds of our enemies fall and among us there is still the benediction of God. No one has yet been touched and we will surely gain our freedom by God's blessing."

But some took it lightly and now they are still there in that country.

**Redemption**

A fortnight later, a messenger arrived from Tangiers with a letter from the merchant Don Louis Buttelaar[101], bringing us the pleasant news that Captain Lambregt, a captain of their High Lordships had ransomed the

[Dutch] slaves that were in Tangiers from the Bashi and he had made an agreement that the slaves who were with the King should be delivered to him within six weeks. I was alone in my tavern when the messenger arrived. I took the letter, but did not open it because it was addressed to the whole Dutch community, but I began to shout and cry without stopping:

"Freedom! Freedom!"

Whereupon, several of my countrymen gathered around. They thought I was mad and extravagant, given that I had not yet even unsealed the letter. No one could read except me alone, for it was in Spanish. I read them the letter, but they did not believe it and I could not make them believe, in spite of the messenger who had brought us the news.

About five weeks later, on the 9th of November, I was summoned, with my husband and the two children, before the King, who granted us all four our freedom and handed us over to the envoy of the Bashi of Tangiers. The King willingly gave us our freedom, but he would have liked to have kept the others, if the envoy had not insisted so strongly on having them as well. On the following day, the King called all the Christian slaves to him and chose another nine whom he freed on the insistence of the Bashi's envoy; he had the others called on the third day, for we were thirteen who had been chosen. And after many difficulties, the King made yet another arrangement, that is to say if the Bashi would send him ten Christian slaves, he would give up the rest, who were ten in all, and thus we would be free, the fourteen that we were.[102]

## Farewells

As soon as the King had given us our freedom, he summoned before him my husband and our little girl whom he liked very much and often played with. My husband could not speak before the King for joy. I knew very well how to pay Turkish-style compliments and my compliments were very fine indeed, so much so that the King was delighted and he broke out saying:

"It is true, as I live, this Christian is worthy to be a princess."

And with this claim to honour, I took my leave of the King.

On the following day, I said my farewells to the mother and the sister of the King. This adieu was as tender as between parents and one of their children. They both wept and once more each gave me two ducats for the journey and they would have liked to have kept me, but it was impossible,

*Tangiers – anonymous print c.1860*

for the King was under an obligation to the Bashi, because he was too weak in terms of men. For Muly Abdela was at Fez, from which he had to oust him if food supplies were to be secure in his empire, and for that reason, the Bashi arrived with quite a considerable army to help the King defeat his enemies.

## The Terrible Journey to the Coast[103]

So we began the journey on the 16th December and we were obliged to make great detours by very unsafe paths to avoid falling again into the hands of Muly Abdela, because then we would have remained in slavery with those who had stayed behind. It was the bad season – wind and rain – with the result that the country was difficult to cross. Every day we were bogged down, up to our knees in mud in the marshes, as were our animals, which sank as far as their bellies. We passed the nights and the days alike in the open and most of the time we didn't have a dry thread on our bodies. I had made myself a tent to spend the nights. Thus we were not out under the stars, but still with no protection against water, for this country has a clayey soil and the earth cannot absorb all the water, so in some places the water was a palm deep. In spite of our efforts to find dry places to spend the night, we were hardly any better off, for the things we slept on were like water and the clothes on our bodies and our covers were the same, so above and below we were in water and it was like being inside a steam bath. My children were sometimes half dead from cold and damp. The difficulties and dangers that we endured during our journey are indescribable.

We arrived at the Bashi's palace on the 30th December and he received us with a salvo of musketry. He provided us with a magnificent tent in which we could pass the night and I was immediately provided with food, of which we had great need. For if I needed anything, I had only to ask the leader in order to be given what I wanted, but this was not the case with the others. I therefore looked after the others vigilantly, for there a woman has more privileges than a man. I was polite and agreeable, with the result that they listened to me attentively and nothing was lacking.

So, on the following day, we continued on the journey with the Bashi and all the army, 100 000 men, or so they said. It is true that it was a considerable army, but I don't believe that there were so many people. We had good weather that day and the journey passed pleasantly to the beating of drums and kettledrums and the sound of trumpets and hautbois[104] and other instruments; and we saw poor peasants, their arms tied behind their backs, stripped and naked[105], walking chained in tens. In the evening, before sunset, we reached a great plain, where tents were set up and where we rested. The Bashi had with him fourteen cannons, which he had fired that evening in the camp, so that we left behind the old year with joy and entered happily upon the new.

On the 1$^{st}$ of January, I wanted to go to the Bashi and ask him for a sheep, but before I could get to the Bashi I had already been brought one. The Bashi having heard me much spoken of was very curious to have a conversation with me, so he had us all brought before him. He spoke to me before everyone and when our conversation was ended, he said:

"Truly, this Christian woman is worthy to be a queen."

I was very polite and agreeable when I spoke and I was as able as the most politic in the country to pay a compliment in accordance with a person's rank. I was very much at ease when I spoke and fearless, so I dared to say things that no-one else in the country would even dare to think. I took my leave of the Bashi who showered all sorts of compliments and blessings on me, for which I thanked him.

Then we set out again on the second day of the new year and continued our journey, not without great dangers, over mountains and through wild regions, forests and valleys and rivers that had burst their banks, and we could not look out for each other, because of the terrible tracks along which we were travelling, which meant that sometimes we completely lost sight of each other. And sometimes we rolled with the beasts we were riding from top to bottom of the mountains and afterwards we rolled again into rivers up to our necks. This accident happened to me often, for having a child on my knees, I had trouble managing my mount. The Moor who was with me was very stupid and did nothing but urge the animal on, so that I often fell into the rivers and slipped down the mountains, which was not without serious danger. My little boy had so many cuts and grazes on his face and hands caused by the roughness of the undergrowth, that he was unrecognizable; and the others had their share too. Those who could walk were unhurt and could find shelter, but me and my little Mietje couldn't and the last evening I really thought that I would never pull through.

We had travelled until late in the evening and we had to guide ourselves by the cries of those who were going on ahead and that was in mountains with steep slopes as high as the sky. My animal, as well as some of the others, could go no further, and there were some who had slipped down from the top of the mountain into the river and just lay there stretched out. My Moor took the reins out of my hands and thus led my mule on the steep slopes and that saved me. Without that, I would have rolled down the mountain with my mule and all. But because of the steepness of the incline and the movement of the beast and the fact I had only one hand to support myself, I slipped backwards off my mule and tumbled down the mountainside three times, with my child in my arms, and remained there stretched out.

This time, I fell on my back which caused me great trouble. I could still just make my voice heard a little, which saved me for they realized that I was no longer on my beast and came to me. Without that, I would have been forced to lie there and I would have been eaten by the wild boar and other savage beasts that roam there in vast numbers. My husband, drawn by the noise, also approached, but it was so dark that I had to be found by sound and by groping around. At last they managed to grab hold of me and take the child, who was half dead in my arms from being hugged so tightly to me, and then they took me down the steep mountainside on my beast, off which I fell twice more, like an arrow from the bow, because of the way the animal jumped when crossing the rivers, which were very high on one side and on the other side very low, so that I was thrown a good eight feet forward and this happened because of the carelessness of my Moor. I thought: this is the last night of my life. I did not want to mount my beast again and I was barely able to walk because of my fall. My husband was furious with the Moor; he gave me back the child and so punished the Moor that he almost gave up the ghost. Then we went on slowly to the village where we spent the night.

The following morning we set out again and once more it was a very dangerous path and they lost another animal with its load on a cliff 25 to 30 feet high and we were forced to go forward on a little track no wider than a big foot that ran along side precipices and from which stones rained down ceaselessly and the animals were forced [sic] to break their backs falling from above with people riding them, for these beasts are accustomed to go straight ahead and it is very difficult to get them to do anything else and so we made our journey in the midst of the greatest dangers.

**Tétuan and the Plague**

At last, towards evening, we arrived at Tétuan, which is still two hours distant from the sea. We were lodged in the house of the English

Consul[106] where we stayed for another three months and five days, for lack of a boat: none came because the death rate was so high. But when we got there, there was no doubt about the plague and the day on which the King freed us, in the town of Meknès, the dead had numbered twenty four thousand and at present there were still fifty or sixty each day. And during our journey, we had passed by various villages and market towns wiped out by death. And about fifteen days before the arrival of our rescuer, the plague reappeared in the town, which made us fear that no one would come to deliver the Christians.

On the 5th of April in the year 1743, a ship came into harbour. The Consul and Don Louis Buttelaar, under whose supervision we found ourselves, headed there at once and when they arrived, they found that it was an English ship, sent here from Gibraltar to learn what the situation in the country was and to make an agreement, because Gibraltar was provisioned from Tangiers and Tétuan. The war between England and Spain meant that the arrival of foodstuffs at Gibraltar from there had been blocked and the plague raging among the Turks was also a reason why life there had become terribly dear and one could get nothing for one's money. That was why this ship had been sent and it brought us news that a Dutch warship had left the roads to come and see whether the slaves from Meknès had arrived. This English ship, having learned that the plague was still raging, immediately set out to sea for Gibraltar and meeting the Dutch ship, hailed it and said that the slaves were waiting for it and that they had already spent three months there, but that the plague was still there. But the Dutch Captain answered that in spite of the plague he would nevertheless act in such as way as to obtain the slaves and he continued to set sail for harbour.

We, however, on seeing that the ship was putting out to sea, felt the greatest dismay imaginable and were filled with the fear that we would be returned again to slavery, for we could not establish what ship it was and we thought it had gone because of the plague raging in the country. However, we were comforted by the return of the Consul and the other gentleman, who gave us accurate information.

That day seemed as long as a year to us, but the night seemed even longer, for the Consul had brought us the good news that our rescuer was about to arrive. On the following day, in the morning, he was already in the roads and the Consul with Don Louis Buttelaar hastened there at once and went on board. But they did not agree on the rations for us other slaves, nor on the repayment of the expenses of the journey, nor on the gifts for the King and his envoy, and there was also the fact that not all the slaves were actually there and on top of everything else there was the cost of our board and lodging for three months, so that the Captain had a great deal of trouble settling all this and so it was not until 11th April that the matter was finally arranged and we could go on board with great joy.

## The Voyage Home

During the days when the negotiations were taking place, we lived in the greatest fear in the world, we could not eat or drink and we perched on the roofs of the houses to be able to watch the boat and all this for fear of a new enslavement. At last, on the afternoon of April 11th we went on board. As soon as I saw the gangplank, I went up it joyfully and so fast that I would even have quite forgotten my children. The joy was so great that it made me burst into tears. I had the feeling that we had all risen from the dead. I, my husband and the children were all admitted to the ward-room table and as the ship was small, with little space, they put us in the sail hold to sleep and during the day we stayed in the cabin. The Captain was called Martinus Meitens[107] and it was he who was in charge of the ship; later he became captain in the service of the States General. Our ship, the "de Brak"[108] had eight pieces of artillery and eight small ships' cannons[109] and a crew of 105 men, with the result that there was not much room for people.

At that time, my little boy was about seven years old and knew how to read, write and speak Spanish as well as the Spaniards, but as soon as he got on board he no longer wanted to speak that language, but he said: "Now I am a Christian."[110] And he never wanted to speak that language again and he has never wanted to speak it, not for promises or threats; my little girl was seventeen months and knew nothing about all this.

It was on the night of the 12th to the 13th that we raised anchor after having paid money for our rations and we crossed into the Spanish Sea[111] and then the Mediterranean. At the end of a month's travelling, we found ourselves back in the Tangiers roads and we fired a canon shot, but received no reply. This caused us much worry on behalf of the other slaves whom the King had promised to send as soon as he had received the ransom money, which made us think that he was no longer [King] and there was another in his place. We lowered the anchor and waited for the reply.

## Attacked by the Spaniards

Meanwhile, the Spaniards of Ceuta[112], seeing this, took us for the English. They arrived in the greatest silence on a moonless night during the watch before midnight, thinking that in this way they could seize the boat. But our lookout men, having seen them in time to give the alarm in all quarters, drove them back off the ship, so that we were well defended. I was with my children in the hold where the sails were stored and could not get them to sleep: hearing all the noise, they thought that it was the Turks trying to snatch us back. I was as they say all fire and flames at not being able to call anyone to look after my children and I would have liked to have contributed as best I could to saving us. At last, the First Mate came close to the trapdoor to call me and ask how we were and I begged him to send one of my fellow countrymen to stay with the children, so that I could help throw the Turks into the sea. Seeing me so inflamed, he said that the people had left the ship, so that I should stay with my children, which bothered me very much, and I could not resign myself to it. So, they drove off the Spaniards and had mercy on them, because they lamented most terribly.

Our Captain had the anchor raised and we set sail towards the Spanish Sea and on the following day we came back to the harbour and the Consul came on board with Buttelaar. They told us that it had been a Spaniard and that the King was still on his throne and that he had only sent four slaves and that he was still keeping six, because they understood the manufacture of guns for the King so very well and he did not want to do without them as yet, but they would do everything possible to get hold of them. So these four arrived on board with the result that we were 18 who had been freed.

## Trouble over a Goblet

Among these four, there was one who had tried to accuse us to the King and we would surely have been burned alive if the King had learned of it. It was a question of a goblet belonging to Muly Abdela that his mother had brought him from the Holy Land of his Prophet Magomet [Muhammad], as a gift for her son and he in turn had given it to his eldest son, who had brought it to me as a pledge in exchange for alcohol to which he was very given. The Law of Magomet, which they greatly venerate, was engraved on this goblet. The four Christians mentioned above went every day to the King and, as one of them needed money and did not know how to procure it, he invented a trick to get hold of this object by the intermediary of one of the King's brothers and accused me of possessing such and such a goblet and of using it for water and other dirty things. If the King had learned this, we would have been punished without any enquiry, but the affair did not go as far as that.

Now, in the year 1742, this is what these Christians told us, that one of the brothers of the King had brought accusations against us to the King and had told him that we had such and such a goblet and that we were putting all sorts of inappropriate things in it and that he had seen it with his own eyes. We were not a little afraid and astonished, knowing the consequences. My husband could hardly say a word, but it was I who spoke up and said that this goblet was back with its owner and that the King could have my house searched but they would not find any such goblet there and I wanted to go with them to the King at once to justify myself, although I would have preferred not to go, but I said it to make it more believable that the goblet had vanished. I pretended that I was furious and that I was absolutely determined to go to the King, but they restrained me, to which I submitted willingly. He left the house and I got the goblet out of my chest and buried it under the ground. We were not unafraid and they likewise, for if they had denounced us to the King and if he had not found the goblet, it would have been their turn and they would have fallen into disgrace with the King. Nevertheless they still invented other new tricks and stratagems to harm us and there was a reason why sometimes I would sing:

"Here it is not the pagans or the Turks who torment us, but we are often tormented by these ruffians and this scum."

Even the Turks were outraged by it and our guard himself was afraid of these scoundrels and had to pretend to endorse them, but then would comfort us thoroughly afterwards, saying that the pitcher that goes too often to the well in the end breaks and that is what would happen to them one day.

While we were on board the ship we had spoken of the matter to the Captain and crew and warned them to keep an eye on them since they were so wicked and thus everyone was warned. They had only been on board a few days when they were up to their tricks again, but they were quickly stopped. But now it was my turn to speak and I got out my goblet and showed it to everyone and said:

"Go on now, find the King and tell him that I have got this goblet so that he can have us burnt."

But Captain Meitens put a gag on them and threatened to put them in irons if they didn't stop making trouble. So they kept quiet until we arrived at Lisbon, where our national boats had a meeting to reprovision after the crossing.

So we arrived at Lisbon on the 20th June to provision, but our tour of duty was not over and I was pregnant and wanted to go to Holland, but there was not another ship heading home and the merchant ships were not able to carry such a large company. Therefore, they put us on shore at Lisbon and sent us to the Dutch Hospital[113] where we stayed for nine days, when another ship entered the harbour; its tour of duty was finished and it had to set sail for Holland and we embarked on it. We had hardly been off the ship three days when these ruffians began their tricks again and tried to strike our inn-keeper dead, which actually harmed themselves, for one of them was very badly wounded in the hand. I was so upset that I was obliged to have myself bled five times in less than a single day. The Consul and the Resident, on seeing this, had two of the main brigands put in prison by the Portuguese authorities, but the most dangerous escaped by means of tricks. But since then he has kept very quiet.

They remained in prison until we embarked on the ship of Captain Samuel Hoogstraten, who had trouble getting them out of prison, which occasioned yet more expense. They came back on board and the Captain reprimanded them severely, so that they would keep quiet and not make trouble.

### Home at Last

So, we set sail, but the weather did not favour us, for we had to sail against the wind and as a result were forced to dock in England at Portsmout [sic], where we re-provisioned. We had already been rationed for several days, since our victuals were exhausted by this long journey. We left Portsmout on the 14th September and we reached Texel safe and sound on the 18th and Amsterdam on the 21st, where I had not been for 20 years. I immediately sought out my fathers [sic] and mother and friends, but they were all dead except for a half-brother, with whom I spent a fortnight, until the time when I accompanied my husband to Medenblik[114] his birthplace and that is where I established myself and still live.

I do not complain at having been so far across the world, nor of my twelve years of slavery, nor of the suffering the Turks caused me, I can rise above that. But the spitefulness and derision that my husband and

I suffered from our fellow-countrymen cannot be forgotten, and it is impossible for me to set it down here in writing.

I sincerely thank the Lord for His grace and I glorify Him for having delivered us out of slavery together with our children, and I hope that our children and our children's children will continue to speak of our adventures in Turkey and it is for that reason that I decided to have them printed, so that everyone can see and read of how wonderfully God protects those that trust in Him, and how He overcomes their enemies and preserves them and what a person can transcend[115], which I have truthfully written down. I hope that the beloved reader will find pleasure here, and remain dear reader.

Your humble, dutiful servant<br>
Maria ter Meetelen

written in Medenblik<br>
On this the 14<sup>th</sup> of June in the year 1748

# Notes

Notes taken from the Hardenberg edition and cited in Bousquet [GHB] are marked [H]; those from *Christenslaven* are marked [L van der B]; the rest are my own.

1. Siktoria. M ter M spelling of names is often approximate. The more standard version has been substituted in the text and her version left in the notes, as an indication of how she heard the names.
2. Perhaps the Claas van der Meer who was baptized there on 4.10.1691 [L van der B]
3. Carmoone
4. Entriana
5. Until 1795 what is now known as Holland was "The Republic of the Seven United Provinces", governed by the States-General, their title was also often translated in the 18th century as "High Mightinesses".
6. St Lucar c.42 miles/67 km from Seville.
7. A smallish, robust fishing or cargo boat c. 20m. long and 75 tons, especially associated with the herring fleet.
8. i.e. Muslim. Because of the dominance of the Ottoman Empire, Turk tended to be used for any non-Christian – Arab, Berber, etc. around the Mediterranean.
9. Small naval cannon or mortar
10. Berlengas archipelago off the Portuguese coast near Peniche.
11. *Anker wyn* – c.39 litres
12. The *rijksdaalder* equalled 2 ½ guilders or approximately 25 grammes of silver, worth c.£15 in 2010.
13. Frans Van der Meer, Ambassador to the Spanish Court [H]
14. A word commonly used for North African Muslims, but M ter M uses it interchangeably with Turks.
15. See Introduction
16. Flemish
17. In the 1730-40s, decorative aprons, often made of the most expensive materials, were high fashion and splendid examples survive.
18. From the crew
19. See Introduction
20. The term used: *verrendeels*, normally refers to the quarter of a herring net.
21. Mequenis, this is quite a standard spelling for the period. Although M ter M uses other variants: Mekenis, Mequenes, etc.

22  *Hoofmeester*
23  Spanish Franciscans, established 1693 – see Introduction.
24  *Bashi*, also written *Basha* by some travellers, is a Turkish title indicating a medium to low ranking military officer, often used loosely for anyone with some authority, It is not to be confused with the very high rank of Pasha.
25  Pieter Jansz or Janse Iede
26  i.e. what generally amounted to hard labour
27  Converted to Islam. The expression was in use in several European languages and, because of the dominance of the Ottoman Empire, Turk was often used as a synonym for Muslim.
28  The Fathers tried to persuade the captives to make wills for the protection of their families and where possible would deliver messages and possessions.
29  Probably the *Credo* or *Apostles' Creed*.
30  In essence, a confession:
"Have mercy upon me, O God
according to Thy loving-kindness
according unto the multitude of thy tender mercies
blot out my transgressions…"
31  Head of all the slaves at Meknès
32  The palaces at Meknès also had vast granaries, storehouses, powder magazines and arsenals. It is not clear which this is. See the Arabic *Chronicle* translated in Appendix 1 for a description.
33  This is obscure. Possibly referring to the Arabic unit of weight - *mann*, which varies widely. M ter M gives it as 10 or 11 lbs. Much less probably, because of the form of the word, it could be *mud* – a Dutch measurement = 168lbs/c.75.6kg.
"*Tak* or *taak* is an old Dutch unit of measurement for liquids" [H]
34  See Introduction
35  A castrated male chicken i.e. eunuch
36  *Khalkhal* – anklets, an intrinsic part of North African dress, often weighing several pounds
37  A number of the details given by M ter M are echoed in the parallel experience of Elizabeth Marsh, captured in 1756 – see Introduction.
38  L van der B suggests *shahada* – the Muslim profession of faith "*lā ilāha ilā allāh muhammadun rasūl allāh* - There is no god but Allah, Muhammad is the Messenger of Allah" repeating which even once was supposed to confirm conversion. Another possibility is the dialect Arabic: *jit* – do it!
39  i.e. the Christians
40  A small silver coin, roughly a farthing. There were 20 to the *gulden* or guilder.

| | |
|---|---|
| 41 | "On the 13th April 1732, Maria ter Meetelen had written him a letter, which was forwarded to the States-General and hence preserved. It provides a summary of what is given here in detail." [H] |
| 42 | Mecca/Maqqah – Muhammad's tomb is in fact at Medina. For more information on the King's mother, see Introduction. |
| 43 | Ramadan began on Feb. 15th, 1732 |
| 44 | L van der B suggests this could be *Allāhu baraka amrak ya sīdī!* – May the blessing of Allah be on you my lord! |
| 45 | i.e. the Spanish and Portuguese cities of Morocco: Ceuta, Mazagan (El Jadida), etc. The English had been forced to leave Tangiers, a European possession since 1471, in 1684. |
| 46 | *Muy* |
| 47 | Perhaps John Leonard Sollicoffre, the English Consul at Tétuan – see Introduction. |
| 48 | *'Id al-Adhar* or *'Id al-Kabir*, the Feast of Sacrifice, which ends the *hajj* season and is celebrated with sacrificing a sheep, in memory of Abraham's sacrifice. |
| 49 | George II of England was of the House of Hannover. |
| 50 | L van der B says that the freeing of the slaves was organized by two Jews, Mattos and Joseph Ribeira (Rebexo) – *Christenslaven* n.108. |
| 51 | Tavilet |
| 52 | *Kāfir* – infidel, unbeliever |
| 53 | Unclear in the original – presumably to avoid some charge or tax. |
| 54 | Meknès was famous for its olive groves – see Introduction – and one of the Christian graveyards was dug up to plant more trees. |
| 55 | A *dubbeltje* was a tenth of a guilder or 25 to the *rijksdaalder*, in other words equal to a gram of silver, valued at c. £1.50 in 2010, but, obviously, with a vastly greater buying power in 1735. |
| 56 | Probably Lalla bint Mulay [H] |
| 57 | Hendrik Lynslager (1693-1768) – see Introduction. |
| 58 | Of the Seven United Provinces The rapid succession of rulers in Morocco frequently caused diplomatic problems of this kind – envoys would find themselves with letters addressed to a deposed ruler and no authority to negotiate with his successor. |
| 59 | M ter M constantly confuses Arab(ic) and Turk(ish), using the latter as a synonym for Muslim. This was common in ordinary speech across Europe, because of Ottoman dominance. |
| 60 | The modern quintal = 100 kgs |
| 61 | The Portuguese were freed for 1025 guilders per person [L van der B n.134] |
| 62 | i.e. doctors |
| 63 | Of the foreign communities |
| 64 | *'Abīd* – the Sultan's black guard –see Introduction. |

| | |
|---|---|
| 65 | *Ciperson* from the Portuguese *quitasol* [H] |
| 66 | Probably Kasba Tadla between Meknès and Marrakesh [L van der B n.137] |
| 67 | Bou Fekran |
| 68 | The word in the text is ditch or moat. In fact the slaves were digging for treasure that the King hoped was buried there. See Appendix 4. |
| 69 | From *matmūra* – see Introduction – here in its original meaning of an underground storage place or granary. |
| 70 | Moulay Muhammad ben Ismaïl, also known as Muhammad ben Arbia. |
| 71 | 75 or 76 freed Spaniards arrived at Cadiz on 7 December 1736, mostly paid for at the rate of 1025 guilders each [L van der B n.138] |
| 72 | *Tarjumān* or interpreter |
| 73 | Apart from the presence of the King's wives, a Muslim would normally be reluctant to touch a pig, but in this case we are told the King has been hunting wild boar, a local sport confirmed by several travellers. |
| 74 | Here, as on various occasions, M de M counts in periods of three months, quarters. |
| 75 | GHB and L van der B both suggest that this is an attempt to render: *a lā intī ghazal, bint ghazal al-akhar* - in other words: "Are you not a gazelle, daughter of another gazelle!" |
| 76 | M ter M gives on various occasions Tanser, Tazer, Tanfer. |
| 77 | For the Guigui or Benguigui family- see Introduction. |
| 78 | Captain Joost Sels – see Introduction. |
| 79 | Here, as in a number of places, M ter M's syntax makes her meaning obscure. |
| 80 | M ter M gives *Paas*, but this is presumably the Muslim *'Id al-Fitr*, or Feast of Fast-breaking at the end of *Ramadan*. |
| 81 | Another case where M ter M's syntax makes it hard to understand exactly what happened. She presumably defends the thieves in the interest of the solidarity of the Christian community and because complaints to the King had a way of rebounding on all concerned. |
| 82 | Mosque. |
| 83 | Perhaps *haratīn* – slaves generally of mixed black and Berber or Arab origin from the southern oases of Morocco or from Mauritania. |
| 84 | M ter M's phrase *naekt en bloot*, literally "naked and nude", sounds odd in the context in modern English. |
| 85 | *Rātib* – appointment, promotion, pay; here perhaps bonus. |
| 86 | The sentence is confused and appears to be negative, which does not make good sense; I have therefore (tentatively) modified it. |
| 87 | M ter M presumably meant leopard. |
| 88 | Another of M ter M's popular sayings, rather obscure today. |
| 89 | Mamooren |
| 90 | Mashra al-Ramal, the army camp set up by Moulay Ismail for the 'Abīd between Salé and Meknès. |

91  It is not clear what this refers to.
92  *Ramadan.*
93  *Dīb* – wolf
94  Mulay Zain al-Abidin bin Ismail
95  Fees, Feest
96  Mulay al-Mustadi
97  *'Arūsat al-sīdī Muḥammad* – the bride of Lord Muhammad
98  Another of M ter M's obscure remarks. Perhaps implying that the Christians were so negligible in the eyes of Allah that they were not even worth chastising?
99  This reliance on the Bible and the fact M ter M ceases to mention the Fathers, suggests that at some point she had abandoned her Catholic faith and adopted her husband's Reformed beliefs. Here she is clearly practising some form of bibliomancy.
100  Psalm 91 verse 7 : "A thousand shall fall at thy side and ten thousand at thy right hand…."
101  Louis Butler, brother of Francis Butler, Consul of the United Provinces at Gibraltar [H]. He reported the arrival of Reuben ben Quiqui at Tétuan with two Dutch slaves [L van der B n.177]
102  The passage is confused, especially the maths. According to H, there is documentary evidence of 14 slaves being freed, see p.144 of his edition.
103  Braithwaite concurs on the appalling road, pp.144-6.
104  The term oboe did not come into use until the late 18th century.
105  Here it is not clear whether they were actually stripped or simply destitute.
106  William Pettieren [H] Probably Pettycrew – see Introduction.
107  Mijtens [H]
108  A man-of-war
109  *Basjes*
110  This again suggests that the family had returned to the Reformed Church to which M ter M's husband originally belonged.
111  Bay of Biscay
112  Seeuta
113  The Dutch had a considerable presence in Lisbon with their own social structures. In 1717, for example, they collaborated with the English in laying out a cemetery for the Protestant community. Much of Lisbon was, however, levelled in the earthquake of 1755.
114  In north Holland, at that date an important town, with a castle and an orphanage with a charming relief over the door built some years after M ter M's return. Assuming the family had converted to the Reformed Church, the Bonifaciuskerk would still seem quite familiar.
115  Lit. "sail back from".

*The Great Mosque at Meknès – postcard c.1900.*

# Appendix 1

## Selected Passages from Al-Nāsirī's *Chronicle*

Maria ter Meetelen, who lived a relatively sheltered life in the *bagnio* of Meknès and was almost certainly unaware of the intricacies of political developments, gives quite a subdued account of the extreme violence that marked the years that she was in Morocco. Al-Nāsirī's *Chronicle* sheds light on what lay behind some of the events she mentions and it therefore seemed of interest to translate a few passages that corroborate or explain her narrative. Christian slaves were of very little interest to al-Nāsirī and are barely mentioned, although he violently objected on legal grounds to the enslavement of Muslim blacks, which was still standard during his lifetime, as it had been a century earlier[1]. Other aspects of his account, however, are in agreement with hers. The examples below also give an idea of the tensions among the various ethnic groups and political factions in Meknès and its environs.

Ahmad ibn Khalid al-Nāsirī (1834-1897), who was from a family of scholars, founders of the Nasiriyya religious order in the 16th century, wrote a history of Morocco and the Islamic West: the *Kitāb al-Istiqsā li-Akhbār duwal al-Maghrib al-Aqsā*. A recent annotated edition in nine volumes was published by Keta Books, Rabat, 2002-7. For the period relevant to Maria ter Meetelen, al-Nāsirī drew heavily on the work - the *Nashr al-mathānī* - of an earlier chronicler, Muhammad al-Qādirī (1712-1773) a retiring and apolitical member of a scholarly family of Andalusian origin from Fez. Details of his life and a history of the text are given in the excellent introduction to Norman Cigar's edition and translation of part of the work *Muhammad al-Qādirī's Nashr al-mathānī: the Chronicles*, The British Academy/Oxford University Press, London, 1981. The following selection was taken from the text published in Archives Marocaines vols IX and X, Paris, 1906 – Dynastie Alaouie du Maroc – *Kitâb Elistiqsâ* part IV by fqîh Ahmed Ennâsiri Esslâouï and translated by Eugène Fumey and the references accompanying each passage are to that edition.

## Moulay 'Abd Allāh [Abdallah][2]

During Moulay 'Abd Allāh's extremely bloody siege of Fez, shortly before Maria ter Meetelen's arrival in Meknès in 1731/1144: "... he allowed them (his troops) to ravage the surrounding countryside, demolish all buildings, cut down the trees and devastate the tilled fields. He then had the rivers blocked, so that the city was deprived of water..." The *Chronicle* goes on to point out that this lead to disaffection and famine, in the largely Berber countryside as well as in the city.

In the course of his campaigns against the Berbers the same year: "..he killed thousands of men and took everything they possessed...."

About the time that Maria ter Meetelen reached Meknès, Moulay 'Abd Allāh, according to the chronicles, decided to destroy one of the most beautiful quarters of the city, Madinat al-Riyād – the City of Gardens - with splendid palaces and numerous public buildings dating from the time of Moulay Ismail:

> "One day of misfortune, the Sultan Moulay 'Abd Allāh mounted his horse early in the morning and from a vantage point on a high hill overlooking the city, ordered the Christians and the Sha'banīya to demolish it. These workmen immediately set about it from all sides, while the inhabitants were still asleep. When they awoke, they saw their houses fall one after another: those who hurried could save their goods and their possessions, but those who had no one to help them or did not make haste to carry away their property were soon buried under the ruins.[3]"

## The King's Mother Goes on the *hajj*

> "That year, he [Moulay 'Abd Allāh] sent his son Moulay Muhammad, who was still a child, and his mother, the Sayyida Khanāta to the Hijāz, to perform the *hajj*. The author of the *Nashr al-mathānī* places this pilgrimage in the year 1143 [1730]. He adds: " The Sayyida Khanāta, daughter of Sheikh Bakkār and mother of the Sultan Moulay 'Abd Allāh, begged her son to allow her to set out for the East in order to accomplish the pilgrimage to the Holy House of Allah. He agreed to this request and provided her with everything that she might need. He had his son Sīdī Muhammad ibn 'Abd Allāh go with her that Allah might strengthen their

affairs in this world and the next. He made the *hajj* with her in the year 1143⁴.

## Roots of Disaffection – the ʿAbīd and the Berbers

Two years later, in 1733/1146, Moulay ʿAbd Allāh sent 15 000 of the ʿAbīd on a punitive expedition against the Berbers. The Berbers succeeded in luring the ʿAbīd into a defile, where they were stripped of everything: "The ʿAbīd returned to Meknès on foot and stark naked." None of them were killed in battle, making the expedition even more shaming. The *Chronicle* goes on to relate that:

"In the year 1147 [1734], the situation between the ʿAbīd and the Sultan Moulay ʿAbd Allāh – may Allah have mercy on him! – deteriorated yet further, for he had killed almost all their leaders in order to avenge their murder of his brother Moulay ʿAbd al-Malik with whom he was on good terms. He therefore caused to die all those who had plotted this assassination; those who had taken part and those who had endorsed it; more than 10 000⁵ ʿAbīd were put to death for this reason. They therefore decided among themselves that they would depose him and put him to death."

This forms the background to the events that Maria ter Meetelen describes in the section "The End of the First Reign of Moulay ʿAbd Allāh – 1731-34".

Two years afterwards, an effort to take revenge on the Berbers ended in the same way and the resulting disaffection is mentioned by Maria ter Meetelen in "The Country in Revolt", as well as a famine, not quite as grave as the one that she describes yet later in 1737-8 - see "Famine".

"The author of the *Nashr al-mathānī* sums up the situation as follows: 'In 1149 [1736 –check] Allah caused all those who had revolted against the Sultan Moulay ʿAbd Allāh to perish: the number of revolts increased, the cost of supplies rose, there was little rain, the population suffered greatly from the high price of food, fat and meat were lacking; at last, many died and as the situation worsened, people emigrated elsewhere⁶.'"

## Moulay Abū al-Hasan 'Alī al-'Araj

It is interesting to compare Maria ter Meetelen's impression of his successor[7], Moulay Abū al-Hasan 'Alī al-'Araj with that of the Moroccan chroniclers:

> "This prince – may Allah have mercy on him! – was forgiving and moderate, and had no taste for blood, Allah protected him to the end of his reign and promised him salvation.
> From Fez, he next went to Meknès where immediately on his arrival he received the oath of the army [*jaysh*]. This is the account as it is set down in the Bustān. I have in my hands the following note written by my paternal grandfather[8]:
> 'On the 1st of Jumada, 1147, the 'Abīd of al-Ramal revolted against the Commander of the Faithful Moulay 'Abd Allāh ibn Ismai'l and withdrew his legitimacy to rule [*bay'a*]. In his place, they proclaimed his brother, Moulay 'Ali, whose mother was A'isha Mubaraka. Moulay 'Abd Allāh left his palace in Meknès, carrying away horses, arms and money, without any battles or fighting. Moulay 'Ali entered the city on the 1st of Jumada II of the same year. Written on the 2nd of the same month by Muhammad ibn Zarrūq – may Allah protect him with His grace!'[9]"

## The Mother of Moulay 'Abd Allāh

On arrival at Meknès, the Sultan received delegations from all the provinces, which brought him their oaths of allegiance and gifts. He thanked them and then distributed all the money he had to the army. He had the noble lady Khanāta, the daughter of Bakkār and the mother of the Sultan Moulay 'Abd Allāh, arrested and stripped of all her possessions. He then had her tortured to force her to reveal any money she might have hidden, but without success. This action was one of his misdeeds - may Allah forgive him! Abū 'Abd Allāh Akansūs says that this Khanāta, who was the mother of Sultans – may Allah glorify them! – was a virtuous, pious and learned woman, who had been taught by her father Sheikh Bakkār. I have seen, he said, her writing in the margin of a copy of Ibn Hajar's *Isāba*[10] witnessed by someone who had certified: 'Without any doubt this is the writing of the noble Khanāta, the mother of the Sultan Moulay 'Abd Allāh.[11]"

This is the queen mentioned by Maria ter Metelen and her letters are quoted by John Windus – see Introduction. It is worth noting that torture to force the revelation of assets seems to have been actually carried out against the Sultan's mother, whereas it was only threatened against the slave.

## The Demands of the 'Abīd and their Consequences

Law and order having broken down, the people of Fez and the 'Abīd decided on a new change of regime and placed Sultan Muhammad on the throne. However:

"The 'Abīd were not content with the money that Moulay Muhammad ibn 'Arbīya had distributed to them, although he had given them everything he had and they demanded more. He therefore allowed them – may Allah forgive him! – to pillage the possessions of the Muslims and he himself had all the grain and provisions forcibly removed from all the houses in Meknès. He had every granary and storage place searched. If he was informed that someone possessed wheat or barley, he had them arrested and they would only be released after what they were keeping back had been handed over. He also seized all the grain that the country people were bringing to the city. Discontent became general and unrest spread everywhere. The people of Meknès left the city. Whoever went out was robbed; the roads were cut and the population found itself in a very difficult situation. Allāh alone decrees what will be![12]"

This was a recurring situation in Meknès and the description concurs with what Maria ter Meeterlen records on various occasions e.g. "The Country in Revolt".

## Attack on the Stables

"Moulay 'Abd Allāh, who had taken refuge among the Berbers, entered Meknès one night with some of his people. He entered the stables, killed all the 'Abīd whom he found there and left after having set fire to their thatched huts."

These stables – presumably royal - were not necessarily the ones where Maria ter Meetelen and her husband kept their tavern, but the anecdote certainly reinforces her stories of urban insecurity even within the palace itself.

The army then set out in pursuit of Moulay ʿAbd Allāh, but were yet again ambushed and trapped by the Berbers. Unable to take revenge on their opponents, the ʿAbīd did what they could to save face:

> "The author of the *Bustān* adds that when they arrived in the vicinity of Sefrou, Moulay Muhammad ibn Arbīya sent a detachment of the army against the helpless inhabitants of the region, particularly between al-Mzadeg and the other villages, to cut off heads, which he then sent to Fez, passing them off as the heads of Berbers! But Allah knows what is the truth![13]"

## Famine and Urban Insecurity

Al-Nāsirī, speaking of Fez rather than Meknès, also confirms Maria ter Meetelen's accounts in "Famine" of theft and famine, and even, on an earlier occasion, cannibalism:

> "Towards the end of 1073 [663], a terrible shortage of food occurred in the Maghrib, which was felt especially in Fez and the surrounding region. People were forced to eat carrion, beasts of burden and even human flesh. The houses were abandoned and there was no one to be seen in the mosques…[14]"

Returning to the period of Maria ter Meetelen, al-Nāsirī continues:

> "At this time [1737], another ordeal no less terrible was inflicted on the populace: famine, unrest and the looting of houses during the night. Wealthy people could not sleep. Almost everyone gave themselves over to theft….The Sultan did nothing to stop this and paid no attention to it.
> A large number of people died of hunger during this period. The guard at the Maristan said that during the months of *rajab*, *shaʿbān* and *ramadān* he had had more than 80 000 people buried, without counting those who had been interred through the care of their families or friends."

He goes on to cite the author of the *Nashr al-mathānī* for the year 1150/1737:

"This year the army [the 'Abīd] that revolted against Moulay 'Abd Allāh was totally defeated after having caused great chaos. The defeat was inflicted on them by the Berbers. The price of food rose enormously; thieves came to attack people at night in their houses: it was no good crying out for help, for nobody answered…"

**Food Supplies Brought in by the Christians**

The same source confirms Maria ter Meetelen's account of food being brought in by the Christians in the section "Famine":

"A large number of people left for Tétouan and the neighbouring regions in order to bring back supplies of grain. It had been the will of Allāh that the enemy infidel should have the responsibility for bringing supplies of food to the land of the Muslims…..One could not obtain food either with money or with any other goods and if Allāh had not entrusted the enemy infidel with bringing provisions of grain to the Maghrib, I believe the entire population would have starved.
This situation was the result of the uprisings and revolts against the kings. Property and goods were not worth a tenth part of their usual price. Allāh did not give back peace to the Maghrib until the day that He chose to recall Moulay 'Abd Allāh to power.[15]"

**Raiding the Storehouses to Pay off the 'Abīd**

Maria ter Meetelen says little about the first period of rule of Moulay al-Mustadī, but al-Nāsirī describes the sending of his half-brother away in chains and, desperate for funds to pay off the 'Abīd, torturing a number of the wealthy to make them give up their possessions. These included an Iraqi *sharīf*, believed to be holding valuables for Queen Khanāta, the mother of Moulay 'Abd Allāh. He ends by saying:

"The Sultan never ceased killing and tyrannizing over his people. He wanted to be compared to his brother, Moulay 'Abd Allāh [16], who, it is true had unsheathed the sword, but he had been very generous, thus making amends for his faults by his munificence. But it was without success, for Moulay al-Mostadī was both avaricious and lacked judgement. May Allah enfold him in His mercy...."

Al-Nāsirī also has some interesting things to say about the storehouses and arsenals frequently mentioned by Maria ter Meetelen, since the Christians were used there as guards and workmen:

"During the reign of this sovereign, the government was very poor and the Sultan constantly had need of money to silence the 'Abīd. He therefore began to rummage through the storehouses of Moulay Isma'il, which no other king before him had thought of touching. He started by emptying the warehouse for iron and sold everything it contained. Then he raided the great godown that held 1000 quintals[17] of sulphur and a great quantity of saltpetre and alum, as well as *baqqam*[18] and other goods, which had been brought to the capital and which came from the spoils taken from the European nations. He sold all that....Next he had the bronze cannons from the forts of the capital dismantled and had them broken up and used the copper to mint coins. But in fact he derived no benefit from all this.[19]"

### Moulay 'Abd Allāh's Expropriations in Meknès

Al-Nāsirī describes the rapid changes of ruler as different power groups managed to install their candidates, albeit briefly. He gives the date of Moulay 'Abd Allāh's return to Meknès as 17 Rajab 1153/6th October, 1740. His behaviour there - as elsewhere, in spite of his mother's efforts to mitigate it - sheds light on some of Maria ter Meetelen's statements about houses being requested and given in an apparently casual way.

"He told his soldiers [the 'Abīd] that whoever wanted a house in Meknès only had to take it. The 'Abīd immediately began to give full rein to their greed at the expense of the people. They came to the doors of the houses and said to the owners: "My Lord has given me your house," or "My Lord has given me your daughter," and the owner had to pay a ransom. It is impossible to describe what the 'Abīd made the people of the city suffer and they were punished and imprisoned if they complained...[20]"

## Moulay 'Abd Allāh Deposed Again

Not particularly surprisingly, al-Nāsirī confirms Maria ter Meetelen's account of events, that after a period of extreme discontent on the part of the people:

"In 1154 [1741], the 'Abīd rose up against the Sultan Moulay 'Abd Allāh and meditated dispossessing him and seizing his person. Warned of their plans, his mother, the noble lady Khanāta, the daughter of Bakkār, left Meknès and fled to Fez al-Jadid. On the following day, her son Moulay 'Abd Allāh set out to catch up with her...[21]"

## Moulay Zayn al-'Abidīn

Not unexpectedly, since they were viewing the situation from diametrically opposed points of view, Maria ter Meetelen and al-Nāsirī were not entirely in agreement over the character of Moulay Zayn al-'Abidīn, whom she calls Muly Sinlebdi - see her section on him - but they both perceived him as an ineffective ruler. Al-Nāsirī states:

"This prince was gentle and generous. He committed no acts of injustice and stripped no one of his possessions, but he had few resources and had to lower the pay of the 'Abīd, which alienated them from his cause, as we will soon see[22]."

From the return of Moulay 'Abd Allāh in 1154/1741 to the time of Maria ter Meetelen's final redemption two years later, al-Nāsirī's account turns away from Meknès and concentrates on the endless struggles between Moulay 'Abd Allāh and his half brothers and in particular on fighting in the Rif.

Two passages have been added, although they do not reflect material given in Maria ter Meetelen: the first because it closes the story of one the *dramatis personae* in her account, the other because it is of interest given the importance of the dynasty's religious mystique in the continued acceptance of 'Alawi rule, a point of which Maria ter Meetelen would not have been aware.

## The Death of Khanāta

"On the 6th of Jumada I [1155/9.7.1742] the noble lady Khanāta al-Mugāfrīya, the daughter of Bakkār and mother of the Sultan – may Allah have mercy on him! – died. She was a woman well versed in religious knowledge and in the literary arts. She was buried in the cemetery of the *sharīfs* in Fez al-Jdid" [23].

## Manuscripts Sent to the Holy Cities

"That year [1155/1742], the Commander of the Faithful, Moulay 'Abd Allāh – may Allāh have mercy on him! – took advantage of the departure of the *hajj* caravan from the Maghrib to the two Holy Cities[24] to send a sumptuous gift, including twenty three copies of the *Qu'rān* in different sizes, covered with gold and scattered with rubies. Among these *Qu'rān* was the great *Mashaf al-'Uqbānī*, which had been handed down in the royal family as an heirloom, as well as the *Mashaf al-'Uthmānī*, which belonged to the Banū Umayya of Andalusia and which had been brought to the shores of the Maghreb by Abd al-Mumin ben 'Ali. We have already spoken at length about this book. The *Mashaf al-'Uqbānī* had belonged to Uqbar ibn-Nāfi al-Fihrī, the illustrious conqueror of the Maghrib. It is said that it was copied at Kairouan from the *Mashaf al-'Uthmānī* and had belonged to various important figures in the Maghrib, until at last it came into the hands of the Sa'adian *sharīfs*. It was on this *Qu'rān* that al-Mansūr made his sons swear to obey their brother al-Sharīf. When it came into the possession of the Sultan Moulay 'Abd Allāh, he had it leave the Maghrib for the Noble Sanctuary: and thus the pearl returned to the land of its birth and the pure gold to its mine. Sheikh Abū 'Abd Allāh al-Masnāwī – may Allah have mercy on him! – said:

"I was able to see the *Mashaf* at that time when Moulay 'Abd Allāh – may Allāh have mercy on him! – took it out in order to send it to the Noble Stone[25]. It seemed to me that the date on his Kairouan copy was debatable, because of the differences that existed between the two."

The Sultan sent at the same time 2700 precious stones in different colours for the tomb of the Prophet....[26]"

1. Bernard Lewis, *Race and Slavery in the Middle East: a Historical Enquiry*, Oxford University Press, Oxford: 1990, p.58-9
2. The westernized form – Abdallah – has been used in the rest of the text to avoid confusion, as it is closer to the various spellings current in the 18th century.
3. Tr. pp.180, 184 and Ar. text IV pp.62, 64
4. Tr. p.181 and Ar. text IV p.62 and see M ter M "Some Help from the Queen".
5. Here, as elsewhere, the numbers are almost certainly indicative not accurate and simply intended to convey a very large quantity, as M ter M herself points out in "The Terrible Journey to the Coast."
6. Tr. pp. 187, 188, 192-193 and Ar. text IV pp.64, 66
7. See section under his name,
8. The *fqih* Abu Abdallah Muhammad ben Qasim ben Zerrouk al-Hasani al-Idrisi
9. Tr.pp189-190 and Ar. text IV p65
10. Ibn Hajar al-Asqalani (1372/773 – 1448/852) was the author of a famous dictionary of the Companions of the Prophet Muhammad *al-Isaba fi tamyiz al-Sahaba*
11. Tr.p.190 and Ar. text IV p.65
12. Tr.pp.197-8 and Ar. text IV pp.67-8
13. Tr.pp.198-9 and Ar. text IV p.68
14. Tr p.113 and Ar. text IV p.69
15. Tr.pp.199-202 and Ar.text IV pp.68-9. Al-Nāsirī' adds: "Here ends the account of the author of the *Nashr al-mathānī*, the *fqih*, the historian, Sidi Muhammad ben al-Tayyib ben 'Abdesalam al-Qadiri. This writer was a witness to the events he describes, for he lived at that period."
16. c.p. M ter M "Moulay Mustadi Deposed."
17. One quintal = 100 kgs i.e.the store held c.100 tons.
18. Probably brazil-wood used as a red dye.
19. Tr.pp.204-6 and Ar. text IV pp.69-70
20. Tr.p.210 and Ar. text IV p.72
21. ibid
22. Tr.p.214 and Ar.text IV p.73
23. Tr.p.217 and Ar. text IV p.73
24. Mecca/Maqqah and Medina
25. i.e the black stone in the Ka'aba at Mecca.
26. Tr. p.218 and Ar. text IV p.74

*The Road to Meknès – anonymous, from John Windus, A Journey to Meknès, London: 1725.*

# Appendix 2

## Letters Exchanged between the English Ambassador, Charles Stewart and the Mother of Moulay Abdallah, relating to the Redemption of Captives.

The Franciscan Fathers at Meknès and other travellers and observers in North Africa comment on the occasions when one group of slaves would attempt to sabotage a redemption that did not include them. John Windus, who accompanied a ransoming expedition to Meknès in 1721, describes a classic example of this behaviour. The mission's Jewish interface, one of the Ben Attar family, suggested applying for help to one of the Queens. This was the mother of Moulay Abdallah, often mentioned by Maria ter Meetelen and al-Nāsirī's Sayyida Khanāta (see Appendix 1). She was clearly at times very influential. Maria ter Meetelen denies this at one point, but also mentions a Frenchman on a ransoming mission courting her favour, ten years later. The letters cited here[1] are interesting in that they make clear both the multiple levels of complexity facing anyone attempting to negotiate at the Moroccan court, as well as the influence exercised by women within the system.

> "*Obstructions to the redemption.* About this time some people who were enemies to peace (particularly the spaniards, and other christian slaves who were there) not being desirous that so many english should be carried away, whose places they must supply, and have a double portion of work; and also grieved to see the king of Great Britain so careful and endeavouring to release his subjects out of slavery, while they lay neglected, and without hopes of redemption: These considerations made them earnestly endeavour to disappoint the ambassador's hopes; and they had prevailed so far in getting the emperor persuaded against it, that he sent a message to the ambassador, telling him, That he believed his master's affairs would require him in his own country, so he was at liberty to return

when he pleased, and that when he came to Tetuan, he might talk with his basha about the redemption of the captives.

But the ambassador perceiving the emperor was about to put him off, consulted how to get the better of this difficulty; and Ben Hattar the jew advised him to write to one of the queens, in a fictitious manner; and as nothing can better show how precarious all negotiations must be, where it is necessary to make use of artifices, and methods of deceiving, rather than inform of the truth, I have inserted the ambassador's letter to the queen.

## Letter to a queen

Powerful Lady, Mother of Muley Abdallah:
The most important knowledge of the authority lodged in your Majesty, I learnt while I was in Lisbon, where endeavouring (as is the custom of all who are to go into foreign countries) to know the persons of greatest power, who can best forward their negotiations, and make relation of them to the king: I met with an old christian, who had been your Majesty's slave two years, and received his liberty by your clemency; and talking with him about my embassy, he informed me that your Majesty was the chief person in this court, who could do me service; for, by your means, my business would come to the ears of his imperial Majesty; and for my better memory, he told me the name of your majesty's mother, the Lady Halima, by whose hands he advised me to convey the letter I should write to your Majesty; which I have accordingly done, asking pardon for my boldness, in following the advice of the said captive, desiring your Majesty to consider the requests I make, and not doubting your approbation thereof, whose protection I promise my self, so that the full meaning may come to the ears of his imperial Majesty for there cannot be wanting in this royal palace a person who can read it.
Upon which dependance I represent to your Majesty, that I came to this court with sincere friendship, and loyal meaning, to kiss the hands of his imperial Majesty, whose honour I had, and in confidence of which, when I arrived at Gibraltar with my sovereign's orders, I wrote to his imperial Majesty, acquainting him with my intention, and the orders of my master the king of Great Britain, desiring him to appoint one of his servants, to treat for a

lasting peace, and redemption of my captive brethren; and also to give leave for me and my retinue to come to this court.

Which letter his imperial Majesty received, and did me the honour to answer, giving me leave to take the said journey with all security, as well for my person as those who should accompany me; and ordered basha Hamet Ben Ally to treat with me for a peace, and redemption of the English captives, as was the custom of the deceased alcayde Ally his father, to be appointed in such cases: which answer pleased me well, and upon sight of it I went to the bay of Tetuan, where I conferred with the said basha, about a peace and redemption of my brethren, in consideration of a quantity of powder, locks, brimstone, cloth, and all the Moors whom we had prisoners: And having treated upon the considerations aforesaid, he asked me to give him time to send a copy of the conditions to his imperial Majesty, to see if he was contented therewith, for if he was not, he could not conclude anything, his imperial Majesty being absolute master therein; which request I told him was very reasonable.

In the mean time, I continued at anchor with my ships in the said port of Tetuan, 'till an answer came with his imperial Majesty, who ordered that the aforesaid agreement should be signed, and sent me a letter (which I have by me) to the same effect, upon which we signed the articles to each other: And at the same time I sent a ship to London, giving an account to my master the king of Great Britain, of the treaty: with a copy of his imperial Majesty's letter, and a letter of the said basha, representing the good inclinations of his imperial Majesty towards us; and also I desire that the ransome might be got ready, with all possible expedition to fulfil the agreement.

With all which the king my master was very well pleased, and instantly ordered the ransome to be got ready, and sent me a writing sealed with his royal seal, and signed with his hand, confirming all that I had done; sending me also a letter to deliver into the royal hands of his imperial Majesty, ratifying and confirming the treaty, which I delivered the day I had the glory to have his imperial Majesty receive my embassy. Also the king my master ordered me to stay a little at Gibraltar (if it was convenient) 'till the said ransome arrived, that I might take it along with me; but if I should go to this court before it came, I should carry with me all the captive Moors, and the present: But the basha being hastened to court, I was obliged to set forward without the ransome, taking with me the present and the captive Moors: And when I arrived at the city of Alcassar, I received news that a ship was come to Gibraltar, with the greatest part of the ransome, only some of the locks were wanting; because they are not made in England but as they are used, unless when there's occasion to send them to Barbary, for which purpose they are now making with all expedition. After that his imperial Majesty had received me with much honour and regard, he gave me nine christians, with liberty to choose them as I pleased; giving me also leave to go into his magnificent palace, whose equal was never seen in the world, and told me that he wou'd dispatch me to my content, and grant all that I asked, being come into his sovereign presence; At which I rejoiced, having the hour to be a mediator between two such powerful crowns, as his imperial Majesty's among Moorish nations, the mightiest; and the king my master's among christians.

To-day being Thursday, I received a message from his imperial Majesty by a renegado, telling me, that he was sensible that I might have business to do elsewhere, in the service of my sovereign, for which reason he desired not to detain me, but I was at liberty to depart after lent; that the nine christians which his imperial Majesty had given me, I might choose them as I pleased, without paying any ransome for them, and about the rest of the captives, I should agree with the basha Hamed when I should return to Tetuan: That the articles agreed upon concerning the sea, his imperial majesty was well contented with; and if anything more was required therein, he would be ready to give me entire satisfaction.

Considering well this message which his imperial Majesty sent, I remained in doubt whether they were his true words, or not well understood by the renegado; nevertheless I answered the said reneado, That concerning treating with the basha of tetuan about peace and redemption of the captives, I thought nothing more remained to do, because upon our treating there before, we had each of us signed the articles of peace, and I had a letter of his imperial Majesty's in my hands, agreeing to what was done; so that nothing further was wanting therein, but that is imperial Majesty would give orders for the Christians, and I would pay the ransome agreed upon, but if there was anything else, about which he would have me confer with the said basha I thought it was not necessary; for since I had the honour to be in his royal court, I would rather explain myself to his imperial Majesty without any mediator; and if there was anything in which I could serve him, I would do it with a great deal of pleasure. Whereupon I beg your Majesty to explain all the abovesaid contents to his imperial Majesty, because in discourse I have not time to do it myself; and if his imperial Majesty will consent to what has been settled, I shall go with great pleasure and honour, to the grief of the enemies of this crown, and of that of my sovereign; but if it should be otherwise, my departure will give joy to the enemies of our countries, and (what I am concerned at) be a means of enmity, when I endeavoured to propagate friendship. Upon which considerations, I hope your Majesty will be pleased to represent these things to the emperor, and use your interest, that I may be dispatched in what for ever remain in all obedience,

Mequinez, july the 20th, 1721

Your Majesty's
most humble and
most obedient servant
Charles Stewart

To this letter the queen sent the following answer, wrote on the back-side.

Queen's answer
To the ambassador who wrote me this letter

I received your letter and what you to me therein have read, and understand your words part by part: I have spoken to my master (whom God preserve) of what you say, without failing to explain to him all in its full meaning: With which his Majesty was well pleased, seeing that never came christian, of more judgement and goodness, to this court, than your Excellency, who in all you say show much understanding and mildness.
Concerning what you tell me of the nine Christians, that my master (whom God preserve) gave you, there is no doubt but it was a present that he made you for a breakfast: and concerning the rest your Excellency says, you may be assured his Majesty will conform to your inclinations, in every thing that shall be proposed.

I know well it is true, that his Majesty was not acquainted with the particulars of the agreement, and quantity of powder, brimstone, and the rest of the things: Because my master thought your Excellency only came here to confer with him, and then to return to Gibraltar to consult with your people, before any thing should be concluded: That was the thoughts of my master.

And concerning the Christians your brethren, who are here slaves, his Majesty knew not how many there were because some of the had turned moors, and other were dead.

But now since your Excellency has declared your design to me, there is no occasion to apply to basha Hamet or any body else; for I will speak to my master (whom God preserve) to the end that he may renow the agreement intirely, and do everything you desire, for in his majesty there is much goodness and generosity. This is my answer.

The mother of Moulay Abdallah.<br>Umelez Ettaba[2]

1. The most accessible edition is the French: John Windus, *Un voyage à Meknès*, édition par Dominique Meunier, Paris: Geuthner, 2005, which includes the English text.
2. Al-Nāsirī calls her "the noble lady Khanāta al-Mugāfrīya, the daughter of Bakkār and mother of the Sultan". She was of the Ourdaia tribe and Moulay Ismail had married her, while in the Sous region of Southern Morocco. She bore him more than one son and her name is given variously as Khanāta, Khenatsa, Ummel Ezz or, as here, Umelez Ettaba, clearly referring to a son or sons other than Moulay Abdallah.

*Portrait of Moulay Ismail – anonymous, from the German edition of John Windus, Reise nach Mequinetz, Hannover : 1726*

# Appendix 3

## A Partial List of the Sons of the Sultan Moulay Ismail as-Samin bin Sharif[1]

Moulay Muhammad al-Alam, *Khalifa* of Montigara 1692-1697, and Sus 1699-1700, rebelled and declared himself Sultan, 1704. He was captured and executed after torture on his father's orders in June 1706. His only son committed suicide in the same year.

Moulay Muhammad Zaidan, *Khalifa* of Meknès 1699 and Cherg 1699-1701. Appointed Heir Apparent for his part in arraigning his brother al-Alam (see above). He was murdered by the women of his harem at Taroudant, October 1707.

Moulay Abd al-Malik, *Khalifa* of Draa. He was executed for plotting against his father, 1696.

Moulay Nasir, *Khalifa* of Draa 1702-1703, and then of Tafilalt. He rebelled in 1711-1712 and was executed by his father, 1714. His eldest son, Mulay Ahmad bin Nasir (Lorenzo Bartholomeo Luigi Trojano), fled to Spain in 1731, he was received into the Catholic Church and baptized in Rome, 4th February 1739. Buyers[2] also identifies a son of Moulay Ismail, as a convert, who took the name of *Don* Pedro de Jesus and petitioned King Louis XIV of France to grant him asylum, 6th November 1708.

Moulay Muhammad al-Mutawakil, executed by his father, 1704.

Moulay Muhammad al-Mutais, executed by his father, 1704.

Moulay Hafiz, *Khalifa* of Cherg 1701-1703, and of Fez 1703-1704, was executed at Fez, March 1704. He had the same mother as Moulay Abdallah, one of the Queens mentioned by Maria ter Meetelen, and al-Nāsirī's Sayyida Khenāta.

Moulay Muhammad al-Muntasir, killed 1728.

Sidi Muhammad Deyfi, executed by his father, date uncertain.

Moulay Muhammad al-Rashid, killed 1736

Mulay Maimun *Khalifa* of Tafilalt.

*Moulay* Abu Merwan, died on the *hajj*, 1717

# Sultans of Morocco from the Death of Moulay Ismail to the Time of Maria ter Meeterlen's Departure

1727         Abu al-Abbas Moulay Ahmad ad-Dhahabi
- Heir Apparent since 1718
- proclaimed Sultan on his father's death, 22nd March, 1727
- deposed in favour of his younger half-brother, 13th March 1728

1728         Marwan Moulay Abd al-Malik
- proclaimed Sultan on the defeat and deposition of his elder half-brother 13th March 1728
- Moulay Ahmad ad-Dhahabi, proclaimed Sultan 3$^{rd}$ April 1728
- deposed at Meknès 18th July 1728
- fled to Fez and arrested there 23rd December 1728
- executed at Meknès, 2nd March 1729

1729 -1734     Abu Abbas Moulay Abdullah [M ter M's Muly Abdela]
- proclaimed on the deposition of his half-brother 5th March
- entered Fez 31st March 1729
- deposed at Meknes, 28th September 1734

1734-1736     Abu al-Hasan Moulay Ali al-Iraj [M ter M's Muly Elle]
- proclaimed on deposition of his half-brother, Moulay Abdullah, 28th September 1734
- entered Fez, 25th October 1734
- deposed 14th February 1736

1736         Abu Abbas Moulay Abdullah [M ter M's Muly Abdela] – for the 2$^{nd}$ time
- proclaimed 23rd May 1736
- deposed 8th August 1736

1736-1738     Abu Abdullah Sidi Muhammad bin Arbia [M ter M's Sidi Magomet Ulda Lariba]
- proclaimed on the deposition of his elder half-brother, Moulay 'Ali al-Iraj, Fez, 8th August 1736
- deposed on the 18th June 1738

1738- 1740     Moulay Muhammad al-Mustadi
- proclaimed on the deposition of his half-brother, Sidi Muhammad, 19th June 1738
- entered Fez, 24th July 1738
- deposed February 1740

**1740-1741**  Abu Abbas Moulay Abdullah [M ter M's Muly Abdela] – for the 3rd time
- restored February 1740,
- deposed 13th June 1741

**1741**  Abu Hasan Ali Mulay Zain al-Abidin [M ter M's Muly Sinlebdi]
- proclaimed on the deposition of his half-brother, 13th June 1741
- deposed, 24th November 1741

**1741-1742**  Abu Abbas Moulay Abdullah [M ter M's Muly Abdela] – for the 4th time
- restored 24th November 1741
- deposed 3rd February 1742

**1742-1743**  Moulay Muhammad al-Mustadi – for the 2nd time
- restored 3rd February 1742

**1743-1747**  Abu Abbas Moulay Abdullah [M ter M's Muly Abdela] – for the 5th time
- deposed May 1743
Restored May 1743 and deposed 1747

**1747-1748**  Moulay Muhammad al-Mustadi – for the the 3rd and last time
- restored July 1747,
- deposed October 1748
- died 1757.

**1748-1757**  Abu Abbas Moulay Abdullah [M ter M's Muly Abdela] – for the 6th and last time
- restored for the last time, October 1748
- died 1757

1  *The Encyclopaedia of Islam* offers a more detailed and accurate account, and a full genealogy is available on line at www.royalark.net. There is also useful information in Norman Cigar, ed and tr. Muhammad al-Qadiri, *Chronicles*, Oxford University Press, 1981, for the British Academy, London. These, as well as other sources have been used for compiling the following list. Each name would be followed by their patronymic "bin Ismail as-Samin".

2  www.royalark.net

*Beato Marco d'Aviano, Preaching and Redeeming Captives – anonymous print c.1700.*

# Appendix 4

## Franciscan Accounts of Meknès at the time of Maria ter Meetelen

Henri Koehler, in *L'église Chrétienne¹*, provides a considerable amount of extremely interesting information taken from the Franciscan archives. Since these are relatively inaccessible, a small amount of his material will be summarised here.

At the beginning of the 18th century, a very important figure for the Christian community in Meknès was Father Diego de los Ángeles, who spent much of his active life organizing redemptions and trying to build some kind of relationship with Moulay Ismail. His efforts were heroic, but not always successful. On one occasion, in 1708, his efforts to free young slaves as well as the elderly led to his being denounced to Moulay Ismail by an old slave, who feared not being included in the redemption, while the young were threatened with death. The result was that he was only allowed to redeem a handful of captives, instead of the 200 he had hoped for and for whom he had paid. Nevertheless, in the period 1692-1724 he was instrumental in freeing 634 slaves.

There were problems of all kinds to be faced. In 1711, Moulay Ismail's son, Moulay Abd al-Malik killed his brother, Moulay Ali. He claimed that he had acted under the influence of alcohol, which may well have been the case, and that the fault therefore lay with the Christians. For a while, the fate of the Community hung in the balance.

The Community's problems were not only with the Moroccans. Bureaucratic manoeuvrings in Spain led to Father Diego first being forbidden from taking individual initiatives – disastrous in a place like Meknès where so much depended on gauging the moment and seizing it - and eventually being recalled. As Koehler bitterly states:

"Gratitude has never been one of mankind's great virtues and in the cloister, just as in the world, the deadening breath of envy, mediocrity and the short term view quickly succeed in neutralizing the efforts of the greatest and the most useful."

Curiously, it was Moulay Ismail, missing the man who had so often been the target of his arguments, rages and threats, who demanded his return.

Another issue was manpower. On July 6th, 1723, the Provincial of the Order, Francisco de la Trinidad, appealed for volunteers for North Africa;

> "The workers are so few that instead of twelve making up the community in Meknès, as there should be, there are no more than seven and several of these are infirm."

A Genoese merchant, Pillet, who had been instrumental in negotiating several redemptions, caused further problems. After being caught embezzling money belonging to one of the queens, he was given the choice between conversion and death. He chose the former and, in his new persona of Abdelady, proved to be no friend to the Christian community.

In 1728, following the death of Moulay Ismail, Meknès was sacked in the course of fighting between Moulay Dahbi and Moulay Abd al-Malik. The convent was looted. The Fathers stripped and herded together – the *'Abid* then hacked at them randomly, killing two and wounding the others. Three weeks later a full account was sent back by the Father Guardian, Manuel del Rosario.[2]

Later, Moulay Dahbi gave the Fathers a little aid, in the form of a food ration. Pillet-Abdelady, suspected by both sides as a *renegado* and therefore perceived as potentially treacherous, was killed and hung upside down from the walls of Salé.

Not long after, the Sultan welcomed a Portuguese redemption, which freed 128 slaves at 475 *piastres*[3] per head and a thousand *piastres* for each of six captive Jesuits among them.

Moulay Dahbi died on March 22nd, 1729, having first strangled his brother Moulay Abd al-Malik. From this time on, the cruelty of the Sultans was no longer what it had been under Moulay Ismail. The *Register of Deaths* less frequently bears the words "killed by the King's hand" and the cross in the margin, indicating a particularly bloody death becomes rarer. Moulay Dahbi himself was only responsible for three deaths, Abd al-Malik for none.

Moulay Abdallah succeeded to the throne. After the Palace revolution of 1734, when the chief of the *'Abid* left the sacred city of Moulay Idris, where he taken refuge, with the tomb cover of the Saint over him for protection, Moulay Abdallah kissed the sacred cloth with great piety, then pierced the chief through it with his spear. It was reported that he wanted to drink the *'Abīd's* blood by way of vengeance.

The *Register of Deaths* relates that on December 23rd, 1735, Pablo de Matta, a deserter from the garrison at Melilla, was offered the choice of apostasy or death. Pablo refused to convert and was ordered to strip and enter a near-by pool of water. The thirty *'Abīd* standing guard were commanded to fire on him. They all missed. Moulay Abdallah seized a gun and hit his target. The story has echoes of the one told by Maria ter Meetelen. The Fathers considered de Matta a martyr.

At the beginning of his reign, Moulay Abdallah was generally relatively mild, however, towards the Christians, although always unpredictable. He forgave a Portuguese who had perpetrated two major thefts, but on the third occasion killed him. He went to discuss the matter with the Father Superior, asking what would have happened in his home country. The Superior answered: "Death", but added: "But it is a pity that you did not allow him time to ask God's forgiveness, for your haste may result in his damnation." The Sultan answered: "O, if he is damned, no matter – thieves deserve to be!" The Secretary of the Franciscan Mission – more charitable, or not wanting to show a fellow Christian in a bad light - wrote in the *Register of Deaths* for April 20th, 1738: "The King killed the Portuguese Andres de Silva with a ball. He received no sacrament, but his exemplary life gives us hope of his salvation."

Moulay Abdallah discussing matters of conscience with the Fathers may seem surprising, but even Moulay Ismail seems to have enjoyed arguments with Father Diego and there is nothing particularly out-of-character about Moroccan royalty enjoying the novel and curious information provided by Maria ter Meetelen.

With time, Moulay Abdallah became more violent and more paranoid. He owed vast sums to the *'Abīd* and knew that they were plotting to depose him. Among other desperate measures, he agreed a number of ransoms and also decided to dig up the Kasbah of Bou Fekran outside Meknès, where legend had it that Moulay Ismail had buried a great treasure. This is the incident described by Maria ter Meetelen in the section "Four Kings in a Day".

Koehler gives the story as follows:

" Abdallah had his slaves taken to the river bed, the course of which twists between marshy banks. Forced labour began in June

1736…The result was not rich coffers, but an epidemic among the labourers. The *Register of Deaths* is unemotional, but paints a macabre picture of the realities of the situation in this year, with the repeated: 'He died three leagues from the Court at Meknès, at the place where all the captives had been taken, at Bou Fekran….' Forty are reported dead, more of course as we know are ill."

Seeing that all his slaves were dying, Moulay Abdallah withdrew them. But he was still 700 000 silver coins[4] in debt to the *'Abīd*.

Moulay Muhammad[5] was considered by the historians as just and generous towards captives, whom he felt should be released after a certain time in slavery. Like his predecessors, he was desperate for cash, which meant that redemptions could be negotiated on not unreasonable terms. The Mercedarians freed all the French, 75 in number, on the 13th of October 1737 and they left in procession singing *De exitu*[6]. The Spaniards followed soon after.

On the 4th of February, 1738, Father Gabriel de Saint-Joseph received the habit at Meknès – the first recorded time that anyone took their vows there.

The various Moulays ratified their favours to the Fathers in a series of *firmans*, for example No.58 in the Archive at Tangiers signed by Moulay Muhammed in 1737, which reads:

"We order you to have anyone who insults the Fathers loaded with chains and that you consider anyone who maltreats the Franciscans or the Christian merchants as an enemy."

1   Henri Koehler. *L'eglise Chrétienne Du Maroc Et La Mission Franciscaine 1221- 1790*. Paris: 1934.
2   This was published in the *Archives* of the Curia of Santi Quaranta, the Spanish Franciscans' house in Trastevere, Rome.
3   Probably the Spanish *peso duro*, equal at this date to roughly 5gr. of fine silver.
4   Probably the *real de ocho*, the Spanish silver coin weighing roughly 27gr. or one ounce.
5   Judging by the dates, this must be Abu Abdullah Sidi Muhammad bin Arbia [M ter M's Sidi Magomet Ulda Lariba] who ruled from August 1736 to June 1738 rather than his successor Moulay Muhammad al-Mustadi, who was on the throne from July 1738 to February 1740.
6   This was presumably Psalm 114:
    "In exitu Israel de Aegipto, domus Iacob de populo barbaro….
    When Israel went out of Egypt, the house of Jacob from a people of strange Language"… (King James version).

# Selected Bibliography

Abun-Nasr, Jamil. *A History of the Maghrib in the Islamic Period.* Cambridge: Cambridge U.P., 1987.
Baker, Samuel. Samuel Baker, *Ismailia* London: 1874, (forthcoming in this series 2011).
Blanc, P.-L. "Earthquakes and Tsunami in November 1755 in Morocco: a Different Reading of Contemporaneous Documentary Sources." *Natural Hazards and Earth System Sciences, Institut de Radioprotection et de Sûreté Nucléaire* (2009): 725-38; on-line at www.nat-hazards-earth-sstst-sci.net/9/725/2009.
Bousquet, G-H, and G W Bousquet-Mirandolle. *L'annotation Ponctuelle De Maria Ter Meetelen.* Paris: Editions Larose, 1956.
Braithwaite, John. *The History of the Revolutions....in the Empire of Morocco.* London: 1729.
Broek, Laura van den, Jacobs, Maaike and Krieken, G. S. van. *Christenslaven.* Zutphen: 2006.
Busbecq, Ogier de. *The Turkish Letters* (1555-1562), tr. E.S. Seymour, Oxford: 1927
Cervantes, Miguel de. *Ocho comedias y ocho entremeses.* Madrid: Viuda de Alonso Martín, 1615; facsimile, Madrid: 1984
Chelebi, Evliya. *Siyyah Nameh* (c.1650), tr. J.von Hammer. London: 1834.
Cigar, Norman. *Muhammad al-Qādirī's Nashr al-mathānī: the Chronicles.* (1665-1756) London: Oxford U.P., 1981.
Colley, Linda. *The Ordeal of Elizabeth Marsh.* London: Harper, 2007.
Crone, Patricia. *Slaves on Horses: the Evolution of the Islamic Polity.* Cambridge: Cambridge U.P. 1980.
*Medieval Islamic Political Thought,* Edinburgh: Edinburgh U.P., 2005.
Dan, Pierre. *Historie de Barbarie et de ses Corsaires.* Paris: 1637.
Dávid, Géza and Fodor, Pál eds. *Ransom Slavery along the Ottoman Borders (Early Fifteenth –Early Eighteenth Centuries).* Leiden: Brill, 2007.
Davis, Robert, C. *Christian Slaves, Muslim Masters: White Slavery in the Mediteranean, the Barbary Coast, and Italy 1500-1800.* London: Macmillan, 2003.
de Groot, Alexander H. *Ottoman North Africa and the Dutch Republic in the seventeenth and eighteenth century* in Revue de l'Occident Musulman et de la Méditerranée, 1985, vol.39, pp. 131-147 and on-line at www.persee.fr
Díaz Borrás, Andrés. *El miedo al Mediterranáneo: La caridad popular valenciana y la redención de cautivos bajo poder Musulmán, 1323-1539.* Barcelona: 2001.

Fanjul, Serafín. *La quimera de al-Andalus*. Madrid: Siglo XXI, 2004.
Friedman, Ellen G. *Spanish captives in North Africa in the early modern age*. Madison: University of Wisconsin Press, 1983.
Garcés, María Antonia. *Cervantes in Algiers: A Captive's Tale*. Nashville: Vanderbilt University Press, 2002.
Haedo, Diego de. *Topographía E Historia General De Argel*. Valladolid: 1612.
Harding, Nicholas. "North African Piracy, the Hannoverian Carrying Trade and the British State 1728-1828." *The Historical Journal* 43, no. 1 (2000): 25-47.
Hirschberg, Haim Zeer, and et al. *A History of the Jews in North Africa: From the Ottoman Conquests to the Present Time*. Leiden: Brill, 1981.
Inalcik, Halil. "Servile Labor in the Ottoman Empire" in A. Ascher, B. K. Kiraly, and T. Halasi-Kun (eds), *The Mutual Effects of the Islamic and Judeo-Christian Worlds: The East European Pattern*, Brooklyn College, 1979.
Koehler, Henri. *L'eglise Chrétienne Du Maroc Et La Mission Franciscaine 1221-1790*. Paris: 1934.
Lewis, Bernard. *Race and Slavery*, Oxford: Oxford U.P., 1990.
Marsh, Elizabeth. *The Female Captive*, (originally published under the name Mrs Crisp, London 1769) ed. Khalid Bekkaoui, Casablanca: 2003.
Mihailoviç, Konstantin. *Memoirs of a Janissary*, tr.Benjamin Stolz, Ann Arbor: University of Michigan Press, 1975.
Milton, Giles. *White Gold: the extraordinary story of Thomas Pellow and North Africa's one million European slaves*. London: 2004.
Miss Tully, *Letters Written During a Ten Years' Residence at the Court of Tripoli* (first published London: 1816), with an Introduction by Caroline Stone, Kilkerran: Hardinge Simpole, 2009.
Motte, Philémon de la. *Several Voyages to Barbary*, tr. Joseph Morgan. London:1736.
Oakley, William. *Eben-Ezer, or a Small Monument of Great Mercy*. London: 1674.
Pepys, Samuel. *The Tangier Papers of Samuel Pepys*, ed. Edwin Chappell, Printed for the Naval Records Office, London: 1935.
Perkins, Roger and Douglas-Morris, Captain K.J. *Gunfire in Barbary*, London: 1982.
Pernod, Hubert (ed.). *Chansons Populaires Grecques des XV et XVI siècles*. Paris: 1931.
Pipes, Daniel. *Slave Soldiers and Islam: The Genesis of a Military System*. Chicago:1981.
Richardson, James. *Travels in Morocco*, London: c.1857.
Rocca, Giancarlo. "La Sostanza Dell'effimero: Gli Abiti Degli Ordini Religiosi in Occidente." edited by Museo Nazionale di Castel Sant' Angelo. Roma: Edizioni Paoline, 2000.
Rodriguez, Jarbel. *Captives and Their Saviors in the Medieval Crown of Aragon*. Washington D.C.: The Catholic University of America Press, 2007.

Saint-Olon, François Pidou de. *Relation de l'Empire de Maroc*...Paris: La Veuve Mabre Cramoisy, 1695.
Shafiq, Ahmad. *L'esclave Du Point De Vue Musulman.* Cairo: 1892. Reprint, Cornell U.P.
Shipman, Pat. *The Stolen Woman*, London: 2004.
Telfer, J. Buchan. *The Bondage and Travels of Johann Schiltberger.* London: Hakluyt Society, 1879.
Thornton, Lynne. *Women as Portrayed in Orientalist Painting.* Paris: ACR, 1994.
Tolédano, Joseph. *Le Temps Du Mellah.* Jerusalem: 1982.
Troughton, Thomas. *Barbarian Cruelty or a narrative of the sufferings of British captives...under Muley Abdallah from January 1746...to December 1750.* Exeter: 1751.
Valle, Pietro della. *I Viaggi Di Pietro Della Valle (C.1616-1623)*, Il Nuovo Ramusio. Rome: Istituto Polgrafico dello Stato, 1972.
Vermeulen, Joos. *Sultans, slaven en renegaten.* Leuven: 2001
Vitkus, Daniel J. *Piracy, Slavery and Redemption: Barbary Captivity Narratives from Early Modern England (16th-18th Centuries).* New York: Columbia University Press, 2001.
Windus, John. *A Journey to Mequinez.* London: 1725.

# Glossary to the Text

*'Abīd* (Arabic) – Black, was the abbreviation for the *'Abīd al-Bukhāri*, the black slave army instituted by Moulay Ismail. See Introduction.

*Allemout* (Arabic) – *al-mudd* unit of measurement, value unclear, M ter M gives it as 10 or 11 lbs.

*Bagnio* (Italian) - lit. bath, used all across North Africa to refer to the slave pens or corrals for the European captives.

*Bailli* (late Latin) – a term used all across Europe for a representative of the ruler – here governor.

*Bashi* (Turkish) - also written *Basha* by some travellers, is a Turkish title indicating a medium to low ranking military officer, often used loosely for anyone with some authority. It is not to be confused with the very high rank of Pasha.

*Basjes* (Dutch) – small naval cannons or mortars.

*Buys* (Dutch) - A smallish, robust fishing or cargo boat c. 20m. long and 75 tons, especially associated with the herring fleet.

Capon (Old Eng., Old French) – castrated cockerel, hence contemptuously eunuch.

*Dīb* (Arabic) - wolf

*Dubbeltjes* (Dutch) – a *dubbeltje* was a tenth of a guilder or 25 to the *rijksdaalder*, in other words equal to a gram of silver, valued at c. £1.50 in 2010, but with a vastly greater buying power in 1735.

*Haratīn* (Arabic and Berber) – of mixed black and Arab descent from Morocco or Mauretania

*Knoo* (Dutch) – used for slave quarters or *bagnios*

*Matamoras* (Arabic or Berber) - From *matmūra*, underground cone-shaped structures, originally used as grain silos, especially in Berber areas of North Africa. They came to serve as the notorious prison-quarters for Christian slaves across North Africa and in Muslim Spain, and were known in the Muslim Kingdom of Granada as *mazmorra*. Slaves were no longer kept in them at Meknès at this date.

*Retep* (Arabic with Turkish pronunciation) from *rātib* – pay, salary, perhaps here bonus

*Rijksdaalder* (Dutch) - equalled 2 ½ guilders or approximately 25 grammes of silver, worth c.£15 in 2010.

*Stuyver* (Dutch) - small coin worth perhaps a penny or five cents.

*Tak* - an old Dutch unit of measurement for liquid.

*Torseman* (from the Arabic *Tarjumān*) - an interpreter or translator, hence the English dragoman or guide

*Vendimi* (Italian or Provençal) - grape harvest

*Verrendeels* (Dutch) - normally refers to the quarter of a herring net.

# Index to the Text

## A

'Abīd 21-3, 25, 32, 133-4, 139-145, 162-4, 171, 173
Agadir (Santa-Cruys) 116
Algiers 3, 7, 10, 14, 18, 22, 29, 39-41, 45, 48, 51, 168
Alkmaar 39, 49
Amsterdam 32, 36, 39, 41, 47, 128
Astrology 99

## B

bandits 97, 98
Bashi *passim*
*basjes* 135, 171
bears 81, 162
Ben Guigui 39
Bible 36, 118, 135
Blacks 13, 20, 23, 66, 104-6, 111, 113, 137
Buttelaar (Butler) Louis, 38, 124, 126
*Buys* 171

## C

Cadix 85, 108
cannibalism 64
Cape St Vincent 39, 49, 51
capon (eunuch) 66, 67, 171
Carmoone (Carmona) 131
Catallana, Jan – head of the slaves at Meknès 61-2, 67-9
Catholics 17, 56
convert 101, 107
Ceuta 15, 21, 133
chains 8, 143, 164

## D

damask 54
death 53, 59-60, 62, 64, 95, 99, 114, 118, 124
    preferred to turning Turk 68
Dekker, Jan Corneliszoon 39, 62
Delft porcelain 85
*diep* 113
doctors 133
dog 37, 51, 53, 62, 66, 77, 82, 90, 95, 98
drums 121
Dunkerque 80
Dutch *passim*
Dutch community 56, 59-62, 119
Dutch hospital at Lisbon 128

## E

eau de vie 81, 90, 109
English 7, 14-6, 28, 29, 32, 34, 40, 63, 79, 123, 124, 126, 133-5, 149, 151, 154, 171
Entriana (Triana) 43, 131

## F

famine 96, 138, 139, 142
Fathers (Franciscans) 10, 26, 28, 29-31, 36, 59-62, 67, 69, 71, 79, 83, 87, 104, 132, 135, 149, 162, 163-4
    (Portuguese) 85-6
Fez (also Fees, Feest) 22, 25, 31, 34, 43, 113-4, 121, 135, 137, 138, 140-2, 145-6, 157-8
Franciscans - see Fathers
French 10, 11, 15, 18, 28-9, 31, 34, 39, 43, 51, 63, 71, 82-3, 91, 154, 164, 171

## G

goblet 126
grapes 109
gun barrel, decorated 83, 87
guns 49, 52, 61, 83, 126

## H

hard labour 2, 8, 30, 132
Holland 1, 14, 35, 36, 38-9, 49, 51, 58, 80, 83, 87, 128, 131, 135
Hoogstraten, Captain Samuel 128
Hospital, Dutch at Lisbon 128

## I

Irish 79, 92

## J

Jansz (also Janse), Pieter "the Fleming"), Maria ter Meetelen's second husband 38, 132
jewels 18, 40, 53, 55, 63, 106, 107
Jewish quarter 32
Jews 31-2, 34, 39, 47, 82, 96, 105, 113-5, 118, 133, 168

## K

*knoo* 171

## L

labour 1, 2, 8, 13, 15, 26, 30, 88, 91, 92, 109, 113, 132, 163
lacquered cabinets 85
lamb 79, 87
Lambregt, Captain 118
lions 30, 81, 101, 104
Lisbon 29, 31, 128, 135, 150
Lutherans 69

Lynslager, Captain Hendrik 39, 47, 83, 85, 86, 133

## M

Madrid 48, 49, 167
Magomet (Muhammad) 64, 71, 118, 126
Mammora 106, 108
Mashra al-Ramal 23, 134
Mass 36, 59
*matamoras* 171
Mecca (Maqqah, Megcha) 16, 71, 133, 147
Medenblik 129
Meitens, Captain Martinus 128
Meknès *passim*
*Mellah* 32, 47, 95, 169
Mequenis 131
mines 18, 21, 89
Moors *passim*
Mother of the King 59, 88, 90, 111-2, 115-6, 138, 140, 146, 154
Moulay al-Mustadi 108, 111, 115
mules 108
Muly Abdela (Moulay Abdallah) 26, 30, 40, 58, 79, 83, 88, 102, 111-3, 121, 126, 149, 154, 157-9, 162-4
Muly Elle (Moulay Ali al-Aredj) 80, 158
Muly Sinlebdi (Moulay Zayn al-'Abidin) 145, 159

## O

olives 90

## P

Parasol 88
passports 49, 51, 55, 97, 105
pearls 18, 63
preserves 81, 87
Pettieren, William 135

plague  116, 118, 124
plants  92
porcelain  54, 85, 87
Portsmout  128
Portuguese  22, 28-30, 49, 72-3, 77-8, 81-2, 85, 91, 108, 128, 131, 133-4, 162-3
Pusole, Jean  82, 83

R

Ramadan  133, 134, 135
ransom  83, 90, 118, 125
ransomed slaves  10, 11, 15, 118
Rebexo (Ribeira)  133
renegades  16, 102
Riperda  37, 39
Romel  23

S

Salé  14, 23, 26, 56, 60, 71, 83, 85-6, 97, 104, 106, 109, 134, 162
Scots  79
Sels, Captain Joos  40, 104, 106, 134
Seville  48, 49, 131
Sidi Magomet (Uld Lariba)  90, 103, 158, 164
Sidi Magomet (son of the King)  116
Siktoria  131
Silla bint Mulay, sister of the King  82
slaves *passim*
Sollicoffre, John Leonard Consul  40, 133
Spaniards  28, 29, 78, 91, 125, 126, 134, 164
stables  25, 26, 70, 141, 142
St Lucar  131
sugar  85, 87

T

Tangiers (Tanfer)  85, 94, 96-7, 124-5, 134
tavern  8, 62, 70, 72-3, 82, 87, 89, 100, 109, 111, 115, 119

Tazer  134
tea  85, 87
tents  106, 113, 122
Tétuan  39, 40, 123, 124, 133, 135
torture  64
Turk *passim*
turn Turk (convert to Islam)  59, 66-8, 82, 92, 106, 116

V

van der Meer, Klaas (Maria ter Meetelen's first husband)  49, 51-6, 58; death of 58-60
*vendimi*  109, 171

W

warehouse  67-8, 76, 78, 80, 87, 108, 109, 113, 116, 144
whales  99
wheat  81, 90, 91, 97, 105, 141
wild boar  94, 95, 123, 134
wine  54, 56, 83, 90, 109

Z

zither  55, 62-3, 66, 68

www.ingramcontent.com/pod-product-compliance
Lightning Source LLC
Chambersburg PA
CBHW031314150426
43191CB00005B/219